TIC: This is China

Living my dream and learning a new culture

Tove Vine

All Rights Reserved 2013. No part of this book may be produced or transmitted in any form or by any means, graphic, electronic or mechanical, including photocopying, recording and taping or by any information storage retrieval system without permission in writing of the author and publisher.

Text Copyright @ 2013 by Tove Vine

ISBN-13: 978-1492993629
ISBN-10: 149299362X

CONTENTS

	Acknowledgments	6
	Preface	9
1	Making a life-changing decision	14
2	Meeting my new city, Guangzhou	26
3	Settling in to Guangzhou	36
4	Training week	54
5	Starting off my teaching career	65
6	Living in Guangzhou	79
7	A new culture	92
8	First Christmas and New Year in China	111
9	Beijing adventures	135
10	Teaching pleasures	144
11	Every day was an adventure	153
12	End of school year	173
13	First anniversary of arriving in China	188
14	Embracing life	208
	Author's Bio	220
	Philanthropy	222

DEDICATION

This book is dedicated to my daughter Elizabeth, who is the wind beneath my wings and in loving memory of my parents Jens and Mary Norup Lund Brix.

*I will give children wings but then I will leave them
alone so they can learn how to fly on their own.
What I am trying to do may be just a drop in the ocean.
But the ocean would be less without that drop.*

ACKNOWLEDGEMENTS

For making this book possible, I wish to thank my daughter Elizabeth for her encouragement and for always being there as my tower of strength and support.

I am also deeply grateful to my dear friend Maz (Marilyn Green Hanson) for lending me a book *Tales of a Female Nomad* written by Rita Golden Gelman, which inspired me to change my life and also for making an "off the cuff" remark in late April 2003 which was to change my life.

I am indebted to my longtime friend Tony Ryan for all his invaluable help, support, as well as his numerous contributions. His unwavering confidence in me encouraged me to finish this book.

My sincere thanks also goes to Helen, my dear friend and coordinator of my school in Guangzhou, China, for her gentle support and guidance, which has helped make my life in China as successful as it is today.

Thank you to Maureen Bella as Preliminary Editor and for guiding me through the first difficult part of putting this book together.

和平

Hépíng - Peace

If you live in China for any length of time you eventually choose a Chinese name. I chose the name

和平

'Hépíng,' meaning 'Peace' to symbolise that I found peace in China—peace within myself and peace in my surroundings.

PREFACE

In 2003, at the age of fifty-seven, I decided to change my life completely. I had a huge garage sale where I was living in Brisbane, sold off a lot of my belongings, put some things into storage or gave other things away. I packed a backpack and went off to China to live and teach English to Chinese children. My daughter was surprised but thought it was great and that I was brave. Some of my friends thought I was a little foolish, as it was the height of the SARS (Severe Acute Respiratory Syndrome) epidemic. My family was not surprised, as I had always had itchy feet!

和平

I was born into a poor family, the eleventh child in a family of thirteen children, in a small village in Denmark. I had six older sisters, four older brothers and two younger brothers. We all lived in a tiny, two-bedroom cottage. My parents were hard-working and taught all their children to work hard. I have a deep respect for my parents, as I understood when I grew up how difficult it must have been for them to raise a family of thirteen kids on a very low income. My father was a labourer and my mother would work in the fields for farmers in the village. It was often very difficult for them to make ends meet.

My father was a very hard man due to the fact that he had been brought up in very harsh conditions. His father died when he was a baby and his mother remarried. Sadly, his step-father didn't like having my father as his son, as he and my grandmother had nine other children. So my father was sent away to live on a farm when he was seven years old to work as a farmhand and had very little education. He even started to smoke at eight years of age, I guess encouraged by the grown-up farmhands.

When my father married my mother, who came from a well-to-do family, and had thirteen children, he worked hard to provide for the family but he also ruled with an iron fist. As we were poor, the only thing my father had to be proud of was his children, and he wanted us to be perfectly behaved wherever we went in the village. Before we left to go to a harvest festival or Christmas party in the community hall, he would line us up and tell us in a stern voice, "When you get there don't talk to anyone, don't look at anyone. You are poor and you are the least important person in the room." I grew up thinking I was worthless because I was poor, and those thoughts would stay with me for many years into my adulthood.

Leaving school before my fifteenth birthday, I managed to get an apprenticeship with a large company in the city close to our village. As I could not get any financial help from my parents, I endured great hardship for the following three years, as often I didn't have money for food or clothes. I had to save my money to pay rent and pay my business college fees.

I had developed a dream of travelling around the world as soon as I had finished my apprenticeship and the first country I visited was England. I obtained a job as *au pair* for a wealthy Jewish family; my main job was to take care of their three children. I went on holiday to Jersey in the Channel Islands with the family and while on holiday I met a tall, handsome Australian man, Gordon, who was to become my future husband. After three years of corresponding, Gordon asked me to come to Australia to marry him—which I did in April 1969.

I worked in Australia in Newcastle, Townsville and Brisbane doing various jobs, including beauty consultant, owner of a squash centre and a gift shop and later as accountant for large companies. Our daughter Elizabeth was born in 1971. My marriage of nineteen years ended in 1988 but I remained friends with my husband, who was a gentle, honest man. He was a good husband and a wonderful father to our daughter Elizabeth. I felt responsible for the marriage break-up, as I was chasing a dream without realising what the dream was.

So, after a life devoted to business and the corporate world, I had had enough. I had always been perfectly dressed and groomed. I had worked hard, and only felt valued if I worked long hours. I was tired. I wanted to find ME. For a long time I felt something was missing in my life. I knew there was another life for me somewhere—a place where I could make a difference, but not until the age of fifty-seven was I brave enough to break away and seek this new life

Since August 2003 I have lived a life full of adventure surrounded by love from my students and respect from their parents. I have made Guangzhou in South China my home, and from there I have ventured out on numerous trips throughout China and Asia. These trips were mostly on my own, connecting with local people as I stayed in the community for a day or a week at a time. Travelling, children, teaching and learning about different cultures are my passions. I am happiest when I am in the classroom, travelling or being invited into other people's lives. I am honoured to be invited into people's homes and lives wherever I go. I am curious. What do they eat? How do they cook? How do they live? I want to know everything.

I have walked over mountains, even been carried down a mountain in a carry chair by two tiny Chinese men, travelled up and down rivers, and slept in five-star hotels, as well as in humble cottages. I have shared gourmet delicacies with wealthy people at expensive restaurants. I have also cooked over open fires in the middle of homes with dirt floors, and later broken bread with the homeowners as their honoured guest. All experiences are equally precious to me.

As a child, I read books about an exotic land called China and dreamt of visiting this land far away. At that time, I also wanted to be a teacher. As a teenager, I dreamed of travelling the world. I wanted to visit every country in the world and learn all the languages in the world—a very ambitious goal, but my idea nevertheless. Today I am an English teacher in China, and I travel extensively to amazing and exotic places. I'm happy to say that I feel my wishes have come true.

1 MAKING A LIFE-CHANGING DECISION

Most men lead lives of quiet desperation and go to the grave with the song still in them. – Henry David Thoreau

I felt this quote applied to me in April 2003. To most people my life must have seemed okay. I was very good at pretending and acting confident and self-assured when in fact inside I felt mostly insecure.

My job in the accounts department of a huge American Company in Brisbane, Australia, was okay but not exciting. I loved the work but didn't feel comfortable in the surroundings where I was working. However, I was too scared to resign because at my age it would not be easy to find another job. So I suffered, and dreamt of another life. I had female friends I met for coffee on weekends and spent time with my daughter Elizabeth, to whom I am very close. She had returned to Brisbane after living, working and travelling overseas for two years. I mostly spent my evenings watching television. There were no men in my life, and I was not looking for a relationship. But I felt life was passing me by. "There has to be more to life than this," I thought.

Once, my dream had been to work in a big company. I studied constantly to improve myself and I did climb the corporate ladder, so to speak, but I was burnt out. A dear friend told me, "You are in the wrong job," but at that time I didn't know what the right job for me was.

On a sunny April afternoon I met a female friend, Maz, for coffee. She lent me a book called *Tales of a Female Nomad*, written by Rita Golden Gelman. From the moment I started reading the book I could not put it down. At every page I said to myself, "I want to do that—I want to live that life." I was so inspired by that book. Rita was writing about how, at age forty-eight, she got a divorce and started to travel around the world.

The next week I met Maz again for coffee and I shared with her how the book had inspired me and that this was the life I wanted. Maz asked me matter-of-factly why I didn't do something about it. Well, for one thing, I didn't have any residual income—I needed to work to be able to buy a few necessities of life like a roof over my head, clothes and food. Then Maz said nine words that were to change my life forever: "Why don't you go to China to teach English?"

Wow! My life changed at that moment! Could I do that? *How* could I do that? My mind was spinning with the possibilities that I could actually do this. I started to investigate, with Maz's guidance.

I searched the Saturday newspaper for an advertisement which would lead me to the TESOL (Teaching English as a Second or Other Language) course which Maz told me I needed to complete. The TESOL certificate is required by many teaching institutions around the world before you can obtain a teaching position. After two hours I finally found a tiny notice titled "TESOL course" and a phone number. I phoned the number at once and booked into a TESOL course for the following Monday evening. The course ran every evening from Monday to Friday and all day the following Saturday and Sunday. On Sunday afternoon I sat for a test and passed. My TESOL certificate was sent to me in the mail a week later.

Holding the TESOL certificate in my hand was a great sense of achievement for me. I had accomplished something. I was thrilled and my feeling of worthlessness due to my lack of education was reduced a little. As I was born into a poor family in Denmark, there had been no money for education, and so all the children in my family left school at age fourteen or fifteen to make their own way in the world.

I had met many lovely people at the TESOL course. We were all seeking the same adventures that teaching English as a second language can bring. None of us knew anything about it yet, but we were excited about the new future we would have.

和平

The day after I finished the TESOL course, I submitted my resume to "Dave's ESL Café" website and within a week I had thirty-five job offers from around the world, mainly from Asia! Within two weeks I had seventy job offers. It was mind blowing!

I had no idea it would be so easy to get a job. It was very exciting to feel so much in demand.

Then came the task of finding the right job for me. First I had to decide which country I would go to and then I had to decide which city. I printed out all the job offers and placed them on the floor in my living room. (I realised later that it was a waste of paper. I felt terrible to misuse so much paper.)

I decided the country I would go to was China. This decision was mainly because I had always wanted to visit China and my research of the different countries showed that the cost of living was very low in China. So, if I couldn't earn a lot of money, I could live very inexpensively in China. That was my logic, anyway. I then discarded all the job offers outside China and set out to investigate the China job offers. I quickly discarded the jobs that paid very little money. Most teaching positions only paid between 2,500 and 5,000 RMB per month (equivalent to $425 to $850[1] in 2003) for a twenty-hour a week teaching job. I started to get a little disheartened, as when I converted the pay into Australian dollars it wasn't very much. However, as

---

[1] The comparison will be made with Australian dollars throughout this book.

the cost of living was so cheap in China, it would probably be okay, I thought.

Finally, I found a job offer which paid 8,000 RMB per month ($1,340) plus an apartment—my heart started to soar! The job was in a city called Guangzhou in the south of China. I had never heard of it—so out came the atlas and a frantic search on the internet and I learnt it is the third largest city in China with a population of some nine million people. The climate is subtropical, and it is the same distance from the equator as Rockhampton in Australia in the southern part of the world. This told me the climate would mean a long, hot summer and a short, cool winter. I replied to the company and a few days later I had a telephone interview at 7 a.m. with an English-speaking gentleman called Aaron—and I got the job! I was so excited.

The company, Nesupia, hires English teachers from the USA, Canada, England, Australia and New Zealand and then supplies primary schools with a foreign English teacher. The primary school children learn English from their Chinese English teacher and also perhaps two or three lessons a week from a foreign English teacher.

I signed a one-year contract with the company. It was only one month after my friend Maz had made the suggestion to me that I should go to China to teach English. Everything happened so quickly.

My daughter Elizabeth was happy and excited for me but also a little worried. "Remember, Mum, you are not twenty-one anymore," she told me. My friends thought I was foolish and were concerned as they watched me pack up all my belongings and put most things into storage after selling or giving away what I didn't want to store.

As the teaching contract was not to commence until September 1st (the beginning of the new Chinese school year), I had plenty of time to get organised. I took a lot of care packing everything in boxes and making sure I labelled each one. I had collected so many useless items. I had thirty-six wine glasses, three dinner sets, three cutlery sets … I could go on and on about all the stuff I had collected! "Who needs all that?" I asked myself. It felt freeing to "de-clutter" and get rid of so many things. I gave most things to my daughter, Elizabeth. I decided in my new life in China I would not hoard. As I was still working, I only had evenings and weekends to pack and have garage sales, so life was chaotic as I prepared for my new life.

和平

I loved going to Chinatown in Brisbane to explore the Chinese shops and watch the Chinese people. I had never been to an Asian country before and didn't know how I would like it. It was so exciting to observe the life in Chinatown knowing that, in a few weeks, I would actually be in China. I would stand close to Chinese people listening to them speaking, trying to pick up words and, hopefully, learning some Chinese words—but that was impossible.

I borrowed a *Lonely Planet* book from the library which covered Hong Kong, Macau and Guangzhou and spent many hours reading about the new city I was yet to meet. I also bought a dictionary to learn some Chinese words to give me a head start.

One day, after visiting Chinatown, I was lucky enough to stumble across the Australia China Friendship Society's office, which is located close to Chinatown. My eye caught a glimpse of a street map of Guangzhou in the window. I was so excited to be able to get hold of a map of the mysterious new city I was to live in for the next twelve months. I spent many hours studying the map and got to know

Guangzhou very well even before I arrived in the city.

I became a member of the Australia China Friendship Society and went to a lovely Sunday lunch where the guest speaker was Wayne Goss, a former Premier of Queensland, whose work had involved strong trading ties with China. I met other people who were interested in the third largest country in the world as well. We all had a different reason to be drawn to this magical country.

和平

August 2003. My last day in Brisbane before I embarked on my adventure was very memorable. Elizabeth treated me to lunch at a lovely restaurant on the river on Coronation Drive and we spent the afternoon driving around saying goodbye to my city. We spent the night in a lovely hotel, as I had already moved out of my apartment.

At the TESOL course I had befriended a lovely couple, Trudee and John, in their early fifties, and also a very nice man, Peter, in his early forties. I called Peter "the gentle giant," as he was tall and had a very gentle nature. Trudee, John and Peter were also hired by Nesupia, and we all decided that we would travel together. We decided to leave on August 15th with an overnight stay in Ho Chi Minh City (Saigon) and arrive in Guangzhou on August 16th. The teachers could arrive two weeks before the beginning of the school year to settle in and become familiar with the neighbourhood in our new city and life in China.

Saying goodbye to Elizabeth at Brisbane airport was difficult. I tried not to cry, as I didn't want to show her that I had some reservations. I didn't want to worry her. I was glad I had Peter, Trudee and John for company after my goodbye hug with Elizabeth.

As I boarded the plane I remembered one of my favourite quotes by Richard Burton, the late 19th Century explorer: *"Of the gladdest moments in human life ... is the departure upon a distant journey into unknown lands."* I felt so excited and had such high expectations for my exploration of a land unknown to me.

We arrived in Ho Chi Minh City at 4 p.m. after a wonderful flight on Vietnam Airlines. After customs clearance, it was 5:30 p.m. and we were taken by minibus from the airport to the inner city hotel where we would stay overnight. As it was Friday afternoon, the traffic was chaotic. The people of Ho

Chi Minh City were going home from work or going out, and the streets were crowded with families on motorbikes. There were often four or five people on a bike: Dad, Mum with baby and a couple of older children squashed between them or perhaps one child in front of Dad on the petrol tank! Gorgeous children with big black eyes and black hair, feeling safe between Dad and Mum—but it certainly didn't look safe to me! I have never seen so many motorbikes and scooters on the road at the same time, and it was an amazing sight. I wished I had a camera to take a picture of streets completely covered by thousands of motorbikes. Fortunately, I visited Ho Chi Minh City again five years later and had the opportunity to take dozens of photos at that time.

The hotel was nice and it was fun to go out in the evening crowd with Peter as my bodyguard (he was 188 cm tall) and explore the part of the city where we were staying. I learned that before you cross the street you have to say a quick prayer—I almost got run over by a motorbike several times! To cross the street in Ho Chi Minh City you must be brave, step out on the road and not stop until you get to the other side of the street. The cars and motorbikes will avoid you. They really don't want to run you down. We walked past many fruit stalls and the smell of the local fruit, durian, was incredible, quite unforgettable. But it was not a smell that made me want to eat the fruit. I was told it is very delicious—if you hold your nose while eating it! I was told the fruit is actually prohibited in some hotels due to the bad smell. I could understand why.

Saturday, August 16th, 10 a.m. We left Ho Chi Minh City for Guangzhou and arrived at Guangzhou airport at 2 p.m. My first sightings of China were fields through a blanket of clouds. My heart skipped a beat, and then as we came closer to the airport I saw the sight of the first high-rise buildings and the Baiyun Shan (White Cloud Mountain) which is right next to the airport. In 2004 a new airport was built one hour north of Guangzhou.

On entering the arrival hall, I knew I was in China because of the large number of people. Getting through customs took a very long time, as there were so many people. Because SARS had recently created a problem around the world, and especially in China, we had to fill in three forms, all relating to SARS. The customs people wanted to make sure we were not bringing SARS back into China.

2 MEETING MY NEW CITY, GUANGZHOU

If you don't take risks, you'll have a wasted soul. – Drew Barrymore

Nesupia Company had notified me by email in Australia before my departure that we would be picked up at the airport by some of their staff, and, sure enough, as I came out of the arrival hall, I saw a lovely Chinese girl holding a sign with my name on it. Two girls, Cloud and Susan, had come to pick up the four teachers from Australia. I liked them at once and over the next twelve months I would develop a lovely friendship with them both. After changing some Australian dollars into Chinese Yuan (RMB) we all piled into a minivan which took us from the airport toward the city of Guangzhou.

My first impression was amazement at how spotless it was. I initially thought it was just the airport that was spotless but as we were driving along the busy main road, a six-lane highway with beautiful landscaped gardens on each side as well as trees and flowers, I learned it was spotless everywhere. According to my research prior to leaving Australia, Guangzhou is also named "The City of Flowers" and "The City of Five Rams." Guangzhou was previously called Canton and is located in the Pearl River delta.

The soil in the delta is very fertile and, according to some sources, is known as the "food bowl of China." It is a city of some nine million people, give or take a few million. No one really knows how many people live in Guangzhou, as there are a lot of Chinese people from the countryside who come to big cities like Guangzhou, Beijing and Shanghai looking for jobs because it is difficult for them to make a living in the small villages. Often the father leaves the family at home in the village and comes to work on construction sites (of which there are many) or as a street cleaner, and only returns home once a year for the Chinese New Year celebrations.

The official language in schools, offices and shops is Mandarin (Pǔ tōng huà) but those born in

Guangdong Province usually speak Cantonese (Guangdong Hua) in their homes and among themselves. The Guangdong people share the Cantonese dialect with Hong Kong.

Guangzhou is the capital of Guangdong Province, which borders Hong Kong, and it has been said that Guangdong province is the factory of the world. For many reasons, it is a very important part of China. It was in the Guangdong province that the Taiping Rebellion and the Opium War started. It is also the home province of the revolutionary leader, Dr Sun Yat-sen (in Chinese - Sun Zhong Shan). He was instrumental in overthrowing the last Emperor Pu Yi in 1911. This area is also important because, in the 19th century, the Cantonese people were the first to leave China in search of gold in San Francisco, Australia and South Africa as well as tin in Malaysia. In addition, it has been said that Cantonese food is the most delicious and the most famous of all the Chinese food. I would have to see if that was true.

Today Guangdong province is very prosperous and Guangzhou has been transformed into a robust economic centre during the past decade. Between 1991 and 1995 real economic growth was about 19% per year. Special economic zones set up in

Shenzhen in Guangdong province are the forces that have helped the economy grow so dramatically. Many multinational corporations are located there. Guangzhou is also the host for several huge trade fairs each year which bring people from all over the world to buy "Made in China" at a very low price.

Guangdong has two seasons: summer from mid-April to mid-September, which is hot, humid and rainy; and a cool to cold winter the rest of the year. The most pleasant times of the year are the months of March and April and also October and November when the weather is neither too hot nor too cold.

Susan, Cloud and I sat in the back of the van and I was so happy and chatty, which they thought was lovely. They laughed at everything I said. As we were driving toward the inner city of Guangzhou I was so glad I had done a lot of research, as I felt Guangzhou was familiar to me. Since I had studied the map of Guangzhou I could recognise famous places on the route from the airport to the inner city such as the China Hotel and the Yuexiu Park with the statue of The Five Rams just across the road. Cloud and Susan were quite impressed with my knowledge of the city. "Have you been here before?" they asked.

"No," I replied, "I just studied the map."

I could see that Guangzhou had certainly moved very fast toward a western lifestyle. There were many cars on the road, especially Mercedes Benz, and I was later to find out that Germany is a strong trading partner with China. There were also many scooters and motorbikes on the road, and the way they weaved in and out of the traffic looked very dangerous to me. The city was very green with many parks and beautifully landscaped flower beds, and a huge number of high-rise apartment buildings. The city of Guangzhou only covers the same area as my home town Brisbane but accommodates about nine million people. If we include two very large suburbs, Panyu and Foshan, the population is as high as fifteen million.

和平

Susan and Cloud took Peter and me to our apartment first. We were very eager to see the apartment, as we didn't know at all what it would be like except that it was a two-bedroom apartment. We were pleasantly surprised when we pulled up in front of the twenty-five-story apartment building and there was a beautiful gate with the name "Fortuna Gardens" on the front. We walked in through the gate, patrolled by two security guards, to a beautifully manicured garden area with lots of potted plants carefully arranged. We heard laughter and splashing and saw a large swimming pool behind a seven-foot high wall, as well as a gymnasium. There were another two security guards in the foyer. I felt secure already after being told there were four security guards on duty twenty-four hours a day. A lift took us up to the second floor and again I was impressed when I saw a very secure door as well as a strong front door leading into our apartment. Our apartment at first glance looked very comfortable. It was not as clean as I would have liked it to be. But I already imagined that a few days of cleaning would get it in good shape. There were two small bedrooms and a large living room, all with air conditioning, a small kitchen and a bathroom with a bath. There was a narrow, enclosed balcony which was really just for drying clothes. There was also a small storage room which came in handy for our suitcases.

We had a lovely view from all the windows. Across a busy highway what first looked like a park I was later to find out was the Guangzhou Zoo (the third largest in China) with many trees and bushes. There was no sight of the animals though, as they were hidden by the trees. For the next four months I would experience being woken up each morning by the animals demanding their breakfast. We were lucky there were no other high-rise buildings close by to block the view. From the living room window we also had a view down to the swimming pool and in the days to follow I would often hear the sounds of laughter from the children enjoying themselves in the pool. I was very glad to see there was a western toilet in the apartment, as I had feared there would be a "hole in the ground" style toilet, also called a "squat toilet."

We put our suitcases in the apartment and then got back in the van again to take John and Trudee to their apartment, which was only a short distance from our apartment. Nesupia would place the teachers in apartments which were close to the schools to which we had been allocated.

John and Trudee's apartment building was also nice, and most of the Nesupia teachers were living in that building. In fact, two floors with twenty apartments were allocated to Nesupia teachers. Sadly for John and Trudee, their apartment on the fourth floor was not as nice as ours. They had two bedrooms and a living room, but only one bedroom was air conditioned. They had no curtains on the windows, even though they looked straight into the apartment across the narrow alleyway; the windows were instead covered with newspapers. It certainly didn't look very nice and was hard for us Westerners to comprehend.

和平

After settling John and Trudee into their apartment we needed to do some shopping. As our apartments had nothing but the furniture, we needed to buy some necessities like towels, sheets and pillowcases before we could retire for the night. Susan and Cloud took us to a supermarket across a very busy road. It was a little scary crossing the road as the traffic in Guangzhou doesn't stop for people on a pedestrian crossing. So it is a matter of jumping between the cars which I became used to very quickly. I have heard of other foreigners who found it impossible to get across the road and simply stopped trying.

After some advice from Cloud and Susan, like where to catch a bus back to our apartment, they left us to do the shopping. Vanguard supermarket was a very modern Western supermarket where we could buy anything we needed. I decided to buy a snack while we were shopping and as we were wandering around the store for a while I started to eat the snack. Very soon, two security guards approached me speaking Chinese, which I didn't understand but they indicated to me that I was not allowed to eat my snack in the store as I had not yet paid for it. They took me by the arm and led me to the checkout where I had to pay for the snack before I could continue to eat it. My Australian friends just stood back and laughed at my dilemma! I had only been in China for three hours and already I was in trouble with the law!

After our shopping spree we easily found the bus stop and got on the right bus. We were told to look for a McDonalds', and to get off at the next stop as soon as we saw the sign. Well, we missed the bus stop and had to go to the next stop, which then meant we would have had a long walk back to our apartment. As we were very tired, we decided to catch a taxi. We had been given a card with the name and address of our apartment in both English and Chinese script, and so we just showed that to the taxi driver and got home safe and sound for a very low fare of 12 RMB (approximately $2).

It was nice to be back in the apartment, as we had been travelling all day and really needed a refreshing shower. The weather in Guangzhou in August was very hot and humid, with a temperature between 30 and 35 degrees Celsius. We were so happy our whole apartment was air conditioned. We spent the evening unpacking and catching up with the news on the CCTV9 English channel. There are about fifty TV channels but only three English speaking channels: two from Hong Kong, Pearl and World, and CCTV9. But I knew I wouldn't be watching much TV because there were so many other exciting adventures to be had in this new city of mine.

We went to bed about midnight and I found the bed much harder than a Western bed. But I slept well and was woken up at 6:30 a.m. by the elephants and lions in the zoo calling out for their breakfast.

3 SETTLING IN TO GUANGZHOU

Every person you meet is a new door opening to a new world.
– Anonymous

Our second day in Guangzhou was a Sunday but that didn't matter, for shops are open seven days a week. That was lucky for us, as we still had lots of household goods to purchase to set up house such as plates, cups, knives and forks and, of course, chopsticks because, after all, "When in China do as the Chinese do." We needed pots and pans because we wanted to do our own cooking—or so we thought. However, when we explored the neighbourhood and found so many cheap eating places where we could get a meal for the equivalent of $1 Australian, we changed our minds.

How exciting it was to walk through the streets and we were amazed how much attention we drew from the local people. I am short with fair skin and red hair and Peter is very tall. The local people stopped and stared at us and we just smiled and said *ni hao* (hello in Chinese), the direct translation of which is "You good?"

At a short walk from our apartment there was a great little 7-Eleven store where we could buy most of what we needed. As we made our purchases, we couldn't believe how inexpensive everything was. I converted every price into Australian dollars and said, "Wow! It is so cheap."

After our shopping, we returned to the apartment loaded up with bags and feeling very satisfied with our purchases. But we felt compelled to rush out into the streets again to soak up the culture. As we wandered around to become familiar with the neighbourhood, we came across a typical Chinese "wet market," which is a style of market where goods have been purchased for generations. It has a dirt floor and vegetables of all kinds—some familiar, some not—are displayed on individual stalls. In the meat stall, meat was laid out on a huge wooden block attracting flies, and chickens and ducks were hung up on hooks or still in their cages awaiting their fate. They were happily clucking away, not realising that their final hour was close.

Cantonese people like their food *very* fresh, and often they will pick out their own poultry and have it slaughtered right there in the market. There were fish, turtles, snakes and prawns swimming around in the not-so-clean water, waiting to be taken out and cooked for the evening meal! As much as I found the wet market fascinating and can appreciate the difference, I much prefer vegetables! I could never buy meat from a place like that. The vegetables looked very fresh and healthy, and so I looked forward to returning to buy some vegetables to cook. Fruit was sold in a special shop and I loved the fruit shops. Guangzhou is in the subtropics (the Tropic of Cancer is one hour by car north of Guangzhou). There was fruit galore—some I knew, some I didn't—but I was sure I would enjoy learning about Chinese fruit which I had not seen before.

As I was wandering through the wet market, I realised that there were no unpleasant smells, not even in the meat and poultry sections. It was certainly interesting to see the difference between the old-fashioned wet market and the super modern supermarket we had visited earlier. The modern supermarket was just like the Western supermarkets where everything is pre-packed and very hygienic. All the staff working in the fresh food and meat sections in the modern supermarkets wore mouth covers and their hair under a hairnet or hat.

As we continued our walk we came across another supermarket and spent some time shopping for other necessary items. I was pleasantly surprised when I found instant Nescafé on the shelf, as I am not a tea drinker and I needed my cup of coffee each day. Nescafé and other brands of coffee were probably mainly for foreigners. Chinese people usually referred to these foreigners as fair-skinned and long-nosed, as well as the Chinese word *laowei*.

和平

Back at the apartment we realised it was actually very dirty, and so we had to buy cleaning products before we could start cleaning. We scrubbed the apartment from top to bottom, which was fun; Peter really got in and cleaned with me. He got up at 6 the next morning and wiped down all the doors and doorframes. After a few hours of cleaning we were happy with the result.

To make the apartment look homey I put on the wall some photos of Elizabeth and of Brisbane. I also put up a big map of Guangzhou so I could look at it often and become even more familiar with the city.

In the first week we had free time to become familiar with the huge city that was going to be our home for the next twelve months. I had signed a twelve-month contract and, to encourage teachers to stay the full twelve months, the company would refund return airfares at the end of that time. I would find out in future months that many teachers did not stay the whole year.

The weather was very hot and humid, between 30 and 35 degrees Celsius, and so I wanted to find some suitable clothes. I was still so amazed at how cheap everything was compared to Australia. I wanted to get to know Guangzhou so I sought out the famous landmarks I had read about in my research prior to the trip. I was also keen to get to know the public transport system as quickly as I could, as I always enjoyed using public transport wherever I went. Most foreigners use taxis in Guangzhou, as it is so inexpensive. Motorbike taxis are also very popular and it only cost 5 RMB (around $ 1) to jump on the back of a motorbike and be taken quickly through the traffic to wherever you need to go—though I was told it can be dangerous.

One famous landmark is the statue of The Five Rams in Yuexiu Park. It is a beautiful huge statue with a legend attached.

Legend has it that in the Zhou dynasty, Guangzhou was also called "Chuting." One year, Chuting was hit by a severe famine. There were no crops and the situation was hopeless. People prayed all day and all night. Their piety eventually moved five celestial beings, and they decided to help the people in Guangzhou. They came down from heaven by riding five goats of different colours, and each of them brought an ear of grain. After they arrived in Guangzhou, they bestowed the grain on the people and gave them a blessing of "No Famine Forever."

From then on, Guangzhou was never hit by famine again and had good weather every year for crops. People lived prosperously ever after because of the blessings the five celestial beings had given them. In order to commemorate the five celestial beings, people built the Wuxian Temple at the place where the celestial beings arrived. This is why the goat is the symbol of Guangzhou. There are many statues of goats in Guangzhou and the Statue of The Five Rams is the most impressive.

I had read about the two best hotels in Guangzhou, The White Swan and The China Hotel, and so I wanted to visit them. I soon learned to travel by subway, as it was so easy and convenient; travelling by bus was more difficult because everything is written in Chinese script. Everything works like clockwork here. The subway is the most modern I have ever seen and it is immaculate. There are cleaners everywhere sweeping and wiping.

The White Swan Hotel was lovely with a huge foyer that featured a beautifully landscaped Chinese garden and a ten-metre high waterfall. I spent some time wandering around this lovely five-star hotel where many foreigners stay when visiting Guangzhou. I saw many sets of white parents with a Chinese baby girl. I became friendly with a mother of a Chinese baby girl and she told me that white parents who adopt a Chinese baby stay at the White Swan hotel for four to six weeks waiting for all the paperwork to be finalised and also so they can get help in case the baby has problems adjusting to their new white parents.

All the Chinese babies I saw looked very happy and contented with their new parents. I was to learn that the parents go to the province where the orphanage is and choose the child themselves. Many parents choose "special needs" children—those with health problems or who need operations—or older children over three years of age. Most of the children that are adopted are girls who have been abandoned by their parents in the countryside, as poor people there still prefer boys to girls.

In the city, I later discovered, it doesn't matter to parents if they have a boy or a girl, but it still matters to the grandparents. I was told by one Chinese girl I befriended that her parents-in-law didn't speak to her for a year because she had a baby girl. Of course with the "One Child Policy," parents in China usually can't have a second child. I was to find out later that there are many variations to the "One Child Policy." It often depends on where your home town is located. For example, if it is a small village in the countryside you may be allowed two children if the first is a girl.

I was told the government introduced this law because too many families abandoned their firstborn baby girl. Usually, in the large cities, only one child is allowed. However, I came to know many women had a second child and then paid a huge fine to the government. With the "One Child Policy" being about twenty-five years old (it started around 1980), the children born under this policy have grown up and are starting their own families. The law is that if a woman and her husband are an only child, they are allowed to have two children. I was to realise over the next many years how complex the "One Child Policy" is in China.

和平

The next day I visited The Garden Hotel, which was within walking distance of my apartment, though along a very busy main street. It is impossible to get across a main street except using the overpass, and there are thousands of these in Guangzhou. There is a fence in the middle of the road to prevent people crossing the road, but I saw many people run across the busy road and jump over the fence because they were too lazy to walk across the overpass. The Garden Hotel is also a beautiful five-star hotel with a huge foyer, and you are welcomed by an impressive golden mural behind the reception desk.

Over the next few days we tried several restaurants where the menu was in Mandarin and no one spoke English. In fact, we met very few Chinese who spoke English at all. They may be able to say "hello" and "bye bye" but that is all. Our first restaurant meal was not a success for Peter. He ordered chicken and received a plate full of chopped-up chicken—head, beak, eyes, feet - the whole lot! He was only able to eat a little, as he said the chicken kept looking at him with such a sad expression on its face! I stayed safe and ordered rice and vegetables. You can't go too wrong with a bowl of rice!

There were very few Westerners in Guangzhou, so we all attracted a *huge* amount of attention wherever we went, what with tall Peter and short me with my fair skin and red hair! People stopped and stared in the street and mothers loved it when I stopped and said *"ni hao"* (hello) to their children.

I love children and the children in Guangzhou are so gorgeous. I cannot walk past a child without bending down and saying *"ni hao."* The children with their lovely brown eyes and delicate features look at me in amazement, and then hide shyly behind Mum or Dad. But after that they are encouraged to say a shy "bye bye," and I blow them a kiss and they blow one back. I am sure they have never seen a fair-skinned woman with red hair before!

It was so wonderful to see the expression on the faces of mothers (or fathers, grandmothers or grandfathers, for that matter, as in China many grandparents look after their grandchildren). They were so excited that a foreigner appreciated and took so much interest in their child. I was to discover over the coming months that many of them wanted me to touch their child, and I was beginning to wonder if there was some kind of legend in China that said it was good luck to touch a short white lady with red hair.

I learned to say *"piaoliang"* (beautiful) as I touched a child and I was rewarded with a huge smile. The older children from about –six to ten years of age loved it when I said "hello" in English. If they were not too shy they would say "hello" back, as they would have learned a little English at school. They always started giggling and ran and hid, but seemed rather proud of themselves that they had an opportunity to speak English, even if it was only one or two words. I was amazed how many said "bye bye" and I was thinking they spoke English until I realised that "bye bye" had been adopted into the Chinese language as a "good bye" and as it was the only English word they knew; it was used as any form of greeting. I was to realise in the months ahead that it is in the smiling face of a child that I find true wonder.

和平

The area where our apartment was located was in a typical Chinese residential area, with lots of high-rise apartment buildings and hundreds of little family-run businesses and restaurants or little eating places at street level. A minute or two walk from the entrance to the apartment there was a restaurant with cheap but excellent food (60 cents for a meal), and a massage place ($5 for a full-body massage—yes, thank you, I will have two a week!) All the masseurs are blind, which I like! When I had my first massage I was surprised, as they even massaged my ears! An amazing feeling! Their loss of one sense (sight) probably heightened their sense of touch.

There was a beautiful square just two minutes away from our apartment. I was told the Communist Party introduced a law that there must be a square for a certain number of apartment blocks in Guangzhou city. Since 99% of the people live in tiny apartments, their only place to exercise is the square. It was wonderful to see the Chinese people really using the square. There are swings for the children and a lot of exercise equipment for the older generation. I discovered that older Chinese people like to exercise their body. They walk down the street swinging their arms or hitting themselves; I guess to increase blood circulation. Walking backwards also seemed to be a popular form of exercise which I thought was strange. There were ping pong tables and a funny circle covered in pebbles. I could not work out what it was for until I saw an old man taking off his shoes and walking around on the pebbles. I realised it was to exercise the balls of his feet. I tried it but it was too uncomfortable for me. Chinese people can put up with a lot more pain and discomfort than Westerners.

There are other ways we are different from the Chinese, and some of these are cultural or from tradition. I realised very early that clearing the throat and discharging the phlegm onto the street is perfectly acceptable in Guangzhou and, in fact, throughout China. I learned very quickly to be observant and jump out of the way! One day I was on a crowded bus and a Chinese man in his fifties decided to clear his throat and discharge the phlegm on the bus floor. However, he was unable to hit a clear spot and it landed on my foot! I was wearing sandals. Fortunately, I had a bottle of water and I quickly washed my foot to remove the phlegm; many people in the bus were looking at me and wondering what I would do. I gave the man an angry look to which he responded with a big smile from an almost toothless mouth. He had no idea he had done anything wrong.

"TIC: This is China." I soon learned to recover from unpleasant experiences by saying quietly to myself: "TIC: This is China." If you want to live here there are things you have to put up with. Walking past a car parked along the curb is also very tricky. Many times I have just avoided being decorated with phlegm coming out of the open window of a car!

In many areas of Guangzhou the footpaths are in desperate need of repair. There are many uneven patches and holes and so it is impossible to walk down the footpath without looking at the ground all the time to avoid stepping into a hole or indeed stepping on a discharged deposit of phlegm. I also quickly learned that the footpaths are not just for pedestrians: many times I was almost run over by bicycles, motorbikes and indeed cars while walking on the footpath. I was to learn in the years to come that motorbikes or scooters, as well as cars, would also make use of the footpath. In fact, a pedestrian is not safe anywhere, it seems. The positive side to all this is that the traffic moves very slowly, so being run over and seriously injured seems to be rare.

和平

I saw many near accidents and was also the cause of a couple of accidents. I was walking down the street in my local area and arousing much interest from the locals, as usual. Two men came along on bikes from opposite directions. They were riding on the same side of the street (not many people follow the traffic laws here). Both looked at me in awe and I could see what was about to happen. I foresaw a crash. I raised my hand, waved and shouted to them, "Watch out," in English, of course. They thought I was waving at them and happily waved back with a big smile. Then there was a bang, and they crashed into each other. I am happy to say they were not hurt, and they just picked up their bikes and off they went.

The following day I walked through a village square and many beautiful little Chinese children were playing on the swings and slides as well as riding their little three-wheeler bikes. Two little girls were looking at me with amazement but kept pedalling, so the bikes kept moving, but they had no eye for anyone or anything else but me. So they crashed into each other and came off their bikes. Even then they were still mesmerised by my looks and they didn't even cry. I rushed to their aid, along with their mothers, and seeing me close up was enough for them to be even more amazed! What fair skin and red hair can do!

It is so much fun to live in a little neighbourhood in a huge city like Guangzhou. As I walked around this frantic city I got very good at avoiding being run down by a car, scooter or bike. It seems as if the cars, scooters and bikes have right of way. They do have pedestrian crossings but they mean absolutely nothing, so I have learned the safest thing to do is to follow a local person and say a quick prayer and that gets you across the street safely. Being very quick is good as well.

A road leads from the main road down to my apartment building, and the further you get away from the main street the narrower the side streets become. On both sides of the street there are small, family-owned shops and sidewalk cafes. After a short time walking that street a couple of times a day, many shop owners came to know me and as I passed by their shop they would come running out on the footpath just to give me a smile and say *"ni hao."* It was so endearing; it really warmed my heart.

和平

Before starting teaching I decided I had to visit the zoo, as it was in fact my next door neighbour; well, across the road at least. The zoo was a great disappointment, as I found the cages were made of concrete, very small and were not clean at all. To me, many of the animals looked unhappy. I went especially to see the panda but sadly that day the panda was ill and in the hospital. As I was wandering through the zoo I noticed a large group of children and adults who started to follow me. I was more of an attraction than the animals in the zoo! The brave children came up to me and shyly said "hello" and asked to have a photo taken with me. Chinese people love having their photo taken and especially with a foreigner.

As I continued to wander through the zoo followed by about fifty children and adults, I wondered if they thought I was a famous person from the West. Who knows?

It was a great surprise to me one day when a little boy came up to me, handed me a rose and said, "You are beautiful." I was so overwhelmed and flattered until I realised that he was a little boy who was part of a big organisation that trains poor children to go into the streets and beg. Instead of actually begging they ask people, especially foreigners, to buy a rose.

I was to encounter these children many times over the next months. They have been taught to be very persistent, so persistent, in fact, that if you didn't buy a rose they would sit down and cling to your leg so you couldn't move. I got caught one day and it was impossible for me to move because the little girl hung on so tightly to my leg. Fortunately, a Chinese street cleaner saw my distress and came with her broom and started to hit the little girl, while speaking to her very harshly. The little girl ran away.

Later I was to discover a trick that would get the children off my leg. I would take out my camera to snap a photo of them and that got them running away very quickly. The first time I did it I had no idea the reaction I would get, I just wanted to take a photo of this little kid hanging on to my leg. I decided to use that trick every time I was in trouble with these children. I am not sure why they run away; I was told it was because they think if you take a photo of them they will die. Another reason is that they know what they are doing is illegal and they do not want to have their photo taken.

4 TRAINING WEEK

Every moment in life is a learning experience. – Anonymous

I never thought I would be so happy in this new country of mine. I took to Guangzhou "like a duck to water." For some reason, the Chinese in Guangzhou thought I was beautiful! I lost track of how many times I was told this. I think that either they had a severe eye problem or they did not know what the word beautiful means! I was told by some of the Chinese staff working at Nesupia that it was my fair skin and red hair that attracted that comment, since this is unusual for them; just as in Western countries dark eyes and olive skin are often considered beautiful. Perhaps it could be because I am a very friendly person and my smile adds to their initial attraction.

It is so interesting for me to have spent most of my life as "the ugly duckling" and come to a country where the people consider me beautiful; I should have come here years ago! Yes, indeed, it was a new life for me and how I needed it to restore my self-esteem! This certainly happened in Guangzhou.

I began to imagine myself in this city for several years. Our Mandarin lessons were to commence the following week. I had already learned many Mandarin words. I had my phrase book with me all the time and I had an arrangement with several shop owners in the neighbourhood that every time I came to their shop they would teach me a Chinese word and I would teach them an English word. I love learning and make it a practice to learn at least one new thing every day. I also believe that it is important to share learning and to engage with other cultures for mutual enrichment. When you choose to go and live in another country I feel it is important to respect the culture and the people of your chosen country. Just because their lives and culture are different from what you are used to from your home country doesn't mean it is inferior; it is just different. Learning about different cultures enriches your experience so much more.

So many wonderful things were happening to me and I was sure it was because I opened my heart to this country and the people. I couldn't stop smiling. I used to bend down and wave and say *"ni hao"* to all the babies and children I didn't see any of the other teachers do that. I decided I would march to the beat of my own drum. I am very strong and I don't do anything just to be part of "the gang." As much as I wanted to be friendly with the other teachers, I didn't want to do things I didn't enjoy or agree with just to be part of the group. I just said no and went and did my own things. I wanted to make it my experience and not the experience others chose for me.

On one of the first evenings we met up with some of the other teachers that lived at Fortuna Gardens. Dave was the manager who looked after the teachers there. Another teacher, Fiona, who had been there a year, had also been made a manager and was looking after the teachers in the other apartment building where John and Trudee lived. The training company, Nesupia, would choose two experienced teachers from previous school years to become managers. Their job was to help the new teachers with adjusting to life in Guangzhou and to teaching in the classroom.

Dave and his girlfriend Sandy (aged in their late twenties or early thirties) were from England but had been teaching English in Egypt and Spain for a few years, and this was their second year in China. Another teacher was Nukas from Nepal, a lovely man in his early thirties who had been in Guangzhou for eight years and loved it. Hugo from Canada was a HUGE man around thirty years old; he was a lot of fun. There were two young girls, Alice and Anna, who were very nice. Adrian was from the USA and Alex was from the UK. They had been there for six months. There were three new teachers from Canada: two gorgeous sisters named Ruth and Cherry, and Ruth's boyfriend, John.

We spent a couple of hours sitting outside Dino's (a tiny eating place) drinking beer or a soft drink and chatting. An amazing thing happened: it started raining, and within thirty seconds the staff had erected a canopy over the tables; it happened so quickly, they were obviously used to doing this! It rained a lot in Guangzhou at this time of the year. I got soaked every day, and so I learnt to wear clothes which I didn't mind getting wet. However, I also bought a lovely raincoat, which was a huge cape with a hood in bright yellow; it was so "cool." I saw this sort of rain cape used by the Chinese locals riding their bikes or motorcycles. The cape is so huge it covers the whole bike as well. I also bought an enormous umbrella—everyone had an umbrella—used for both the sun and the rain.

和平

The next morning we met Dave in the foyer of the apartment building and he escorted all the new teachers to the Nesupia office. We caught a bus but I was sure in the future I would not use the public transport as it was only a pleasant, thirty-minute walk. At the office, I finally encountered the squat toilet for the first time! It was not as uncomfortable as I thought it would be, and I soon got used to it.

We had a great day meeting the administration staff, and they were all very nice. As well as Cloud and Susan who had picked us up from the airport, there was Olga, who always had a beautiful smile on her face, and Mary and Sara. They were all lovely young Chinese girls and very happy and willing to help us. At my first meeting with the administration staff I gave all the girls a gift: an Australian pen and a small toy kangaroo and koala. They all appreciated my gesture.

All the teachers arrived one week before the school year started on September 1st, as we had to spend a week in training. In 2003, Nesupia had a total of thirty-seven teachers from the USA, Canada, England, Australia and New Zealand. The company had contracts with approximately thirty primary schools in Guangzhou and the surrounding suburbs to supply a foreign English teacher for one to three English lessons a week. On the first day we received valuable information about living in China, and especially in Guangzhou.

Dave and Fiona were running the day and the whole week would be taken up with organising visas, getting bus passes and phone cards, learning where to shop, and the best markets. But as I had done so much research and we had been there a week, I knew most of this already. During the week-long course we would learn how to teach the children, so it was an exciting week. We all had a teacher's assistant (TA for short), which was a young Chinese girl or boy who would help us with everything, including picking us up from the apartment and taking us to the schools where we had to teach. I was really looking forward to meeting mine.

The program we would be teaching was excellent. It was called *Sesame Street,* with the characters from the PBS TV Show. The students loved the program, especially Big Bird, Bert, Ernie, Cookie Monster and all the other characters. Before the school year started I would decorate the classroom with large cut-outs of most of the characters.

We were teaching kindergarten as well as primary school children from Grades 1 to 6. I was allocated Grade 1 and 2 classes—a total of six classes—as well as four kindergarten classes.

和平

The owner of Nesupia ruled the company with an iron fist and all the staff was very scared of her. The foreign teachers were constantly amazed at the harshness of the working conditions. The teachers' assistants worked there because they wanted to use what English they had already learned and improve their skills so they could get a better job in the future. The assistants were paid only 1,000 to 1,500 RMB (between $165 and $250 a month) for a very long working day.

The week of training was relaxing and it was fun getting to know all the young teachers and assistants. Every lunch hour, a group of us would go to a little sidewalk café and eat typical Chinese food, which was not at all like the Chinese food I used to eat in Brisbane. I would try to order noodle soup with no meat—*bu rou*—but one day I saw something unfamiliar in my noodle soup. I asked the owner what it was. The answer didn't please me. It was pig's ear sliced very thinly! I had heard that Chinese food in China is different from Chinese food outside China, and it certainly is! There are hundreds of tiny sidewalk cafes selling quick take-away meals which are very popular for workers. They either buy their take-away lunch or sit at the low tables and chairs on the footpath eating noodle soup, or rice with some kind of meat and vegetables. Many sidewalk cafes serve pig intestines and chicken feet, which are both great delicacies in Guangzhou. The pig intestines looked like wide pieces of noodle. I felt no need to try either of those delicacies! A quick meal is very cheap, 3 to 4 RMB (less than $1). It was almost not worth cooking yourself.

I was the oldest of all the teachers. My Australian friends, Trudee and John, were in their early fifties and Peter in his early forties. There was a Canadian teacher, Betty, in her early fifties, who had been there five years. Jenny was thirty-two, also from Canada and had been in Guangzhou for four years. She was married to a Chinese man, Larry, from Tianjin, the harbour city near Beijing. Since Betty and Jenny were experienced teachers and had lived in Guangzhou for a long time, they took the new teachers under their wing. There was another long-term teacher from England named Heather who also married a Chinese man and had a baby daughter, but later divorced. It was interesting to note how many teachers had been with Nesupia for many years.

Sitting in the meeting room at Nesupia surrounded by all these young people and feeling part of the group was an amazing feeling for me. I felt so young and alive. I had been worried that the younger teachers would exclude me because of my age but that was not the case. Some of the teachers included Sean, Sam and Ray from Canada, all nice young men and a lot of fun. A good looking Canadian teacher named Steve became a very good friend and I enjoyed spending time with him. We would sometimes go and have a Sunday lunch together at a nice restaurant. I was so honoured that those young people wanted to be friends with me.

和平

At the end of the training week we were allocated our school and classes, and I was so lucky to be given one of the best primary schools in Guangzhou, the Dong Feng Dong School. I was allocated three Grade 1 classes and three Grade 2 classes. I was also given four kindergarten classes in a kindergarten near the school. Each Grade 1 and 2 class had three English lessons a week and kindergarten classes had two lessons. So I had a total of twenty-six classes per week. Each class was forty minutes and so my working week was less than eighteen hours in the classroom. Compared to my working week of sometimes sixty hours a week working as an accountant in Brisbane, this job was almost like a holiday!

In the one-week orientation course we learnt how to teach and were given many examples of how to deal with the students. We would have twenty-five students in each class, which is half of the normal Chinese class. A question we were asked was, "Will you scream at the students?"

As a new teacher I said, "Of course not; I would never scream at the students." This reply was met with a smile from the experienced teachers. Without words they were saying, "We will see!"

I was allocated a young teacher's assistant. Her name was Viola and she was nineteen years old but looked thirteen and behaved like a thirteen-year-old. She wasn't very mature for her age.

The Nesupia Company treated all the teachers and assistants to a fantastic "beginning of the school year dinner" at a big, well-known restaurant. It was interesting to see all the teachers and assistants together enjoying an evening of excellent Chinese food. It was fun to try all the new food which I didn't know. I would ask Viola, "What is this?" and her answer was always the same: "Try it and you will find out." Sometimes she didn't know what it was either!

5 STARTING OFF MY TEACHING CAREER

When you educate a child you empower them - how can that not be an honourable occupation? – Anonymous

The first day at Dong Feng Dong School was exciting. I was a little nervous, as I had never taught children before. I had taught many adult classes at various times during my life on special subjects. I taught Danish at James Cook University, Townsville as well as teaching make-up techniques during the years I was working as a beauty consultant. I also spent time teaching business development. But I had never been faced with twenty-five six and seven-year-olds before. My first impression was how sweet they were, and the second was how noisy and naughty they could be! Dong Feng Dong School is a very expensive and well-known school, and only parents who have a lot of money can afford to send their child there. So all the children were from wealthy families and each one was an *only child*.

As an English teacher in China it is a normal process to assign English names to the students. So the first lesson was taken up with giving the students English names and nametags. I needed the students to have nametags, as I wanted to be able to call them by their English names often so they could get used to it. A few children already had English names for various reasons. For example, if they had attended a kindergarten where they were taught by a foreign English teacher they would have been given an English name. Sometimes parents may even have given their children English names if they had lived overseas. So the fun began finding English names for most of the students. I listened to their Chinese name and gave them an English name that sounded like their Chinese name. As I had ten classes, each with twenty-five students, that came to two-hundred and fifty students for whom I had to find English names!

Of course I could double up on names in the different classes. Mostly I would give the students

English names with only one or two syllables, as it would be easy for them to say and also remember. In each class I wanted to name a little girl Elizabeth, as that would be a reminder of my daughter back in Brisbane. I named a sweet little girl—rather overweight but so cute—Elizabeth, then I had to teach her to say the long name, as it is a four-syllable name and difficult to say for a Chinese child. After leaving the class she came back and held the nametag up to me, indicating that she wanted me to pronounce Elizabeth again. I said, "Your name is E li za beth." And she whispered, "E li za beth, E li za beth." It was sooooo sweet. My heart would melt as I looked at those gorgeous kids.

Another little girl who stood out was a gorgeous Grade 1 student who spoke perfect English. I was wondering why but didn't have a chance to ask her during the lesson. She already had an English name, Selina. After the lesson she came up to me, tucked at my T-shirt to get my attention and said in the sweetest voice, "Miss Tove, do you want to know why my English is so good?" Of course I wanted to know. She said, "I lived in New Zealand for four years." This gorgeous little girl was to be my student for the next nine years until she went to Australia (Sydney) to continue her high school education. I had the pleasure of seeing her grow up from a little girl to a beautiful teenager, and we also became very good friends.

However, as all the children are from very wealthy, one-child families and they are fed a lot of sugar (all the commercial bread sold in shops here is very sweet), they are naughty and hyperactive. So my TA Viola and I had to be strict in order to control them. I learnt the first day that I had to scream, "Be quiet!" at the top of my lungs to get them to be quiet and listen. I remembered that I had said earlier that I would not scream! It hadn't taken long! The silence would last for two minutes and then they would start talking again. The first time I had to shout I scared myself, as it was so against my nature to raise my voice. Before that time I do not think I have ever raised my voice to anyone in my entire life.

和平

The next few weeks were also lovely experiences in the classrooms with the students. They were so gorgeous but often so naughty. They love to have fun, and so to keep their attention I would play lots of teaching games. I also set up a system to keep them motivated to be good and participate in the lesson. I formed two teams and the students had to work as a team, which is important in the Chinese school system. So if one student in the team was good and answered questions, the team would get a point but if a student on the team was naughty, the team had points taken away. I gave each team a name; one team was the Kangaroo team and the other team was the Koala. I had brought small toy kangaroos and koalas from Australia and so the students on the kangaroo team were given a kangaroo and the students on the koala team a koala, which they promptly hooked on to their school bags.

The students loved the competition. I personally didn't like team competition because I thought it was unfair to good students when other students on the team were naughty. Later I set up a better system to keep the students motivated and individual students would benefit from being good and work hard. All the students would get a stamp on their stamp sheet if they did their homework. When a student had ten stamps they would get a sticker next to their name on a poster displayed in the classroom. At ten stickers they would get to earn a gift. Most of the students worked very hard to have a sticker and eventually a gift. The gifts I would give would be a small kangaroo or koala which I had brought from Australia. Sadly, they were made in China, probably in a factory close to Guangzhou!

I was fortunate that my classroom was on the ground floor right next to the kitchen. Other teachers had their classrooms on the fourth or fifth level and had to walk up many flights of stairs.

I usually started to teach at 10:30 a.m. in the morning and had two lessons before lunch. My TA and me would then eat lunch and have a rest in the classroom and then continue with two or three lessons in the afternoon.

The students would eat lunch in the school. They would line up at the little window outside the kitchen (next to my classroom) with their little stainless steel bowl and get some rice, fish, scrambled eggs or other types of food served into their bowl. The food was not appetising. I sometimes ate the food but did not enjoy it at all. After lunch the students would sleep on their desk or on a chair for an hour. I couldn't believe my eyes when I first saw the little students sleeping in this way. I worried they would fall off and hurt themselves and I was told that that does often happen. The students didn't seem to care.

The kindergarten I was allocated was very old, and I was surprised to see how dirty it was. It was a boarding kindergarten where the students would live from Monday to Friday and only go home for the weekend. I found it very difficult to understand that little three-year-olds would not see their parents for five days. However, they seemed to adjust to it after a while. The first few weeks were very difficult, as I was teaching little children who had just started kindergarten and the lesson was at 9 a.m. Monday morning. They had only just arrived and had said goodbye to Mummy or Daddy, which they didn't want to do. So they were crying and missing their parents during the lesson. For the first two to three weeks all I could do was to try to stop them crying by playing games with them with a puppet. Not only was kindergarten new to them, but they also had to face a white person, and I am sure most of them had never seen such a person before. So I had to hide my face behind a puppet and talk to them with a funny voice.

Eventually, after a few weeks, most of the students settled down and began to take part in class activities and learn some English words and songs. I taught them from an excellent English book for kindergarten students called *Tiny Talk*. It was about two little bears named Benny and Sue and their

Mummy and Daddy. The first words they learnt were, "Good morning, I am Benny. Good morning, I am Sue, Mummy and Daddy," and they had lovely songs to sing with each unit in the book.

和平

The next days and weeks of teaching would be wonderful. I felt so happy and comfortable in the classroom and the children liked me so much, which was wonderful. They were always trying to get close to me so I could show them some affection. I tried as much as I could to accommodate their needs, but I was also aware that I couldn't show some students affection and not others, and so I tried to spread it around. Fortunately I am a very affectionate person so it was easy to show these gorgeous children the affection they sought.

They were so proud to show me off to their mother, father, grandmother or grandfather after school when I met them at the school gate.

One day a lovely little girl Laura came up to me as she came into the classroom and said, "You are beautiful." I was sure she had practised that sentence! Another day a boy called Darren gave me a pendant with a profile of Chairman Mao. He was too shy to give it to me himself and so he asked

Viola to give it to me. I put it on my chain straight away and he saw it around my neck as soon as he came into the class room and his face lit up like a Christmas tree! He was so proud that I wore it.

Another day I wore white slacks and a white T-shirt with Chinese writing on it. The writing was actually old Chinese script and was an advertisement for a museum exhibition. My assistant Viola could read it. I thought it was a rather amazing coincidence that a shirt I bought from St. Vincent de Paul in Brisbane fourteen years earlier for $2 (as a sun cover for a day yacht sailing in Moreton Bay outside Brisbane) was now being worn by me in China and people could read the script. Could this represent the merging of my past and present lives?

After a couple of months with Viola as my TA, I requested a new assistant as Viola was very young and couldn't control the students. I was given a new TA whose name was Patty. Patty was twenty-eight and had a son who was five years old. She was a very experienced TA who knew how to control children. The classes were much easier once working with Patty as my TA. I was able to focus on teaching and not controlling the students, and the teaching became so much more enjoyable.

Some of the lessons were lots of fun. One day I had to teach the students a unit in the book about looking after a pet, especially a dog. So I bought a gorgeous toy dog with long, brown ears as well as everything needed to set up a vet surgery. I brought to the class room two bowls for water and food (the bowls were from my kitchen and I bought a box of little biscuits as food), a big bowl to bathe the dog in (from my kitchen), a brush to brush it with (my hair brush), some shampoo to wash it (a little bottle from my bathroom), a ball to throw to it (new tennis ball) and I used my gold belt as a lead to take it for a walk! I brought in my Chinese white shirt for one of the children to wear to dress up as a vet. I also brought in a first aid kit with a homemade stethoscope (a bottle top with two pieces of string) to listen to the dog's heart, a tiny screwdriver to use as a needle to give an injection and a magnifying glass to check it's ears. There were also band-aids, a thermometer, a bandage, a pill bottle, plastic and white gloves and finally a facemask. This is how I set up a vet surgery.

The students took turns being the 'owner' of the dog, giving the dog food and water, a bath, brushing him and taking him for a walk. They threw him a ball and took him to the vet for an examination.

It was wonderful and the children loved it. Patty was *very* impressed that I had gone to so much trouble. She told me that I was a wonderful teacher. It warmed my heart, as I really wanted to be an excellent teacher.

和平

During the next few weeks I enjoyed my teaching, both in the primary school and the kindergarten. I considered myself so fortunate, and I treasure those lovely interactions with the students. I became more and more comfortable and confident in the classroom. We were only two months into the school year and already several teachers were leaving. Many of the younger teachers came straight from high school, college or university. They were spending a year travelling and teaching in China and they were not used to working. Consequently, they found the long working hours difficult. Most teachers would have twenty-five hours a week in the classroom but then we had to spend time doing lesson preparation. Altogether, though, the working hours were less than the normal thirty-eight- or forty-hour working week in Western countries.

Two of the teachers who left were a Canadian couple, Drew and Angel. Drew got sick and spent a week in hospital and that experience was so bad that two days later he flew home and Angel followed one week later. A Canadian girl, Cherry, left to work at The Garden Hotel. But, unfortunately for her, Nesupia would not release her from her contract and so she had to return to work for another month to fulfil her contract. If you leave to work for another company before your contract expires, the company can blacklist you and not release you, which means you can't get a work visa to work for another company.

I was happy with my working conditions. I was offered more teaching hours on Friday evenings and Saturdays and I gladly accepted them. I never complained and so the Chinese girls in the office were happy to help me anytime I needed it. They were very obliging: if a teacher got a cold or had any other medical problem the girls happily gave advice in regard to what medication to buy or they even went with us to a doctor or hospital to translate.

I took on a job also with Nesupia on Friday evenings teaching students whose English was more advanced than that of their classmates. It was called "A Reading Club" and I would read a book with the students, discuss the new words and teach them correct pronunciation. That proved to be an excellent opportunity for me in terms of my future in China.

Another teaching job I was allocated by Nesupia was in a kindergarten in an outlying suburb on Saturday morning. My TA was a friendly young girl named Kerry. We would catch the bus to the suburb, which took two hours, and then a taxi to the kindergarten, which was a thirty-minute ride. It was a beautiful, huge, new kindergarten with lots of large classrooms and sleeping areas for the students as well as lots of outdoor playing areas. It was a boarding kindergarten, and so the students would sleep at the kindergarten from Monday to Friday and only go home on the weekend. However, they would come back to the kindergarten on the Saturday just for the one-hour English class. It was rather amazing to imagine those tiny two-and-a-half and three-year-olds being away from their mother and father for five days. It made me realise what Chinese families have to endure and how difficult it must be for them. I thought back to my own childhood, which was very poor as there were thirteen children, but at least we had our parents with us all the time.

After teaching three classes on Saturday morning, we had to get back to the bus station to catch a bus to another kindergarten, where I was to teach another three classes on Saturday afternoon. Since the kindergarten was so far from the centre of town, a taxi would not come and collect us, and so two of the teachers had to take us to the bus station on their small motorbikes, this proved to be rather scary, as they weaved in and out of the traffic at great speed. At times they even rode their motorbike *against* the traffic! I wanted to close my eyes I was so scared, but my adventurous spirit wouldn't let me.

6 LIVING IN GUANGZHOU

Every day brings the promise of a new beginning, hope and discovery. – Anonymous

Over the first few weeks I became good friends with Jenny, Larry and Betty. They were all very kind and helped me to adjust to my new life in Guangzhou. Jenny took me shopping to amazing places and showed me how to get good bargains.

They also invited me to go to church one Sunday morning in September. There is a non-denominational church in Guangzhou called Guangzhou International Christian Fellowship. The church is held every Sunday morning in a conference room at the Star Hotel. No Chinese are allowed (by order of the Chinese Government). It was a lovely gathering of people from all over the world, and there were a lot from Nigeria (China has strong trading ties with Nigeria). Through the church I would meet many new people and make friends. We would have lunch in a restaurant at the Star Hotel after the service, which cost $8 for an all-you-can-eat Western-style buffet and fantastic food.

One Sunday during the service we received sad news in regard to the church. The Chinese Government would not renew their licence, as the church had become "too big" (approximately two-hundred and fifty members). Also, the Star Hotel said they no longer wanted to rent a function room to the church. I guess they wanted to play it safe and not support a group the Chinese Government did not want to recognise.

The church had to break up into smaller groups of not more than thirty people per group. Then the government would issue a licence to individual groups who would have to meet in private homes. Everyone seemed to have a positive attitude about this; it was a chance to start afresh. So I thought it would be interesting to be part of this change. It almost felt like a return to the origins of Christianity and celebration in small house churches. However, it would give me a chance to meet other foreigners – though it would not help my learning of Chinese.

The Nesupia Company made an announcement after the first couple of weeks that they would pay for Chinese lessons for all the teachers. I was so excited at the prospect of starting to learn Chinese, actually Mandarin. Amazingly enough, only eight out of the thirty-seven teachers took up the offer of Mandarin lessons.

The Chinese teacher was very good, but I found it to be more difficult than I had expected. However, I struggled on and was able to lay down a good foundation for my future study of this difficult language. I understood a little then of how hard it was for the Chinese to learn English.

和平

One Sunday in October, Nesupia was invited to enter their foreign teachers in a "Friendly Sports Day" to compete against the Guangzhou local government employees; the foreigners against the locals. There were other foreign companies that had been invited as well, so there were a large number of people. There were three sports: soccer, tennis and orienteering. I was chosen for orienteering and we were driven by bus to a mountain on the outskirts of Guangzhou just next to the airport. Yes, a mountain next to the airport! Probably not very safe I would say, but I was told they were building a new airport at some distance from the mountain.

It was a beautiful mountain called Baiyun (White Cloud) with hundreds of walking tracks and picnic spots and a fantastic view over Guangzhou (when the pollution is not too bad). It was a very popular spot for the people of Guangzhou to visit during weekends. I noticed that the beautiful parks and other outdoor areas are very much used by the Chinese; I guess it is because 99% live in apartments and going to parks is the only way of getting some exercise. It is also a good way for them to feel grass under their feet and "smell the grass and the flowers," so to speak. Baiyun Mountain is also called "the lungs of Guangzhou," as it is where the local people go to get away from the pollution of the huge city with millions of cars, buses and motorbikes.

We were all given a smart, new red T-shirt and a small hand towel and arrived on top of the mountain to be briefed about our challenging task of navigating around the mountain. I was excited, as I love navigating and reading maps and I think I am rather good at it. I know men sometimes think women can't read maps, but I can.

I was partnered up with Peter, my "bodyguard," and to our great surprise we came in first of all the foreigners and second overall. A Chinese team beat us, but they knew the mountain well, as it was their usual Sunday walking outing (well, this is our excuse!). We were so amazed and surprised and we had no idea how we won! I guess we just read the map and followed it to the best of our ability. The next team arrived back at least thirty minutes after us. For our efforts we received a lovely trophy, which I promptly gave to Ms. Wang (the Director of Nesupia) to place in the office. It was presented to us at the end of the day in front of hundreds of people on stage at a sports arena where all the local government officials were represented.

We were entertained by a dragon dance and a "ladies' fan dance," both of which were very colourful and beautiful. Different nationalities entertained us by singing songs from their homeland and the teachers from Nesupia sang the Beatles song *With a Little Help From My Friends*, with the line about singing out of tune. We rehearsed five minutes before we went on stage, so you can imagine how professional it was! Well, we weren't too bad; at least we sang loudly and hopefully nobody noticed that we sang out of tune! We got generous applause anyway. It was altogether a wonderful day for which I am very grateful, as once again I made lovely new friends.

Chastity, the lady who organised the orienteering, was a stunning young Chinese lady who for some reason took an instant liking to me and wanted to be my friend. I also met her mother, a lovely little Chinese lady who was just delightful. I was invited to have dinner with them, which meant I had to find a few spare hours in my busy schedule! I also made friends with a fantastic young Chinese man named Alan and his girlfriend Joanne. Alan was a twenty-one-year-old university student. It constantly amazed me that young people could be bothered speaking to me, but I have been told there is a saying in Chinese that roughly translated into English is: "It is a great honour to be in the presence of an old wise person." Isn't that wonderful?

Alan's parents lived in a little village three hours by bus west of Guangzhou and he invited me to come home with him to visit his parents. He said, "My parents would love to meet you." That was to be another adventure. He also offered to be my personal guide when I went to visit a wonderful area called Guilin, which is well-known to foreigners because it is so beautiful. I have been told that three lakes and two rivers flow through the mountain area and this creates brilliant scenery. I have yet to do my research.

This is an email I received from my new friend Alan, who was still learning English:

20 October 2003

Dear VINE, Tove,

This is Alan; do you feel so surprised that I write to you so soon? Ha-ha (smiling), yes, I want to give you a big surprise, and I hope you can receive and read this letter ASAP, then I can attain my object. It's really a fantastic day today, because I can make friends with you, make friends with many many others, that's great, people should regard each other as his friend or family, then the world will become more beautiful, and there will be no wars, no pain. I tell you a secret, you are not the first foreigner I chat with (because I chatted with my foreign teacher before). But you are the first foreigner I write to, now I'm so excited and don't know what to say, but I will give you a brief introduction to myself. My Chinese name is Ye Feng, my family name is Ye and the word Feng in Chinese means mountains, I guess that my parents chose this name for me just want me to be the top man as high mountains. You know, my English name is Alan, do you know why I choose it as my English name, the answer is so easy and funny, because I think this name is easy to write and sign, that's crazy, isn't it. I come from a northern city called Shaoguan, also in Guangdong (Canton) province, which is not so far from Guangzhou, and it's a very beautiful city famous for its mountains and waters, if you ask your Chinese counterparts, I think most of them have been there before. If you are willing to go there and time permitted, I'm ready to be your personal tour guide and safeguard, haw-haw. I love playing football and listening to music, but most of the time I will prefer to internet surfing. Ok, since this is the first letter I write to you, appropriate length of the letter is important, so in order not to interrupt your work, I think it's time to say goodbye. See you! I'm looking forward to your quick correspondence, and wish you every day is a happy day.

Yours sincerely,

Alan Ye

And another wonderful email from Chastity, who was also still learning English:

Oct 20, 2003

Dear Tove:

It is a miracle for you to accomplish the mission with so remarkable record yesterday in Baiyun Mountain. Congratulation once again! It worth a lifelong memory for us all! I want to tell you that you are really like my angel mother, so sweet and generous. You are the most lovely woman I have ever seen besides my mother. It is so lucky I am to be in the same city with you. Both I and my mother would love to make friends with you. Please feel free to call me. You are always welcome to be our guest. My home number is xxxxxxxx. Please say hello to Peter for me. He is really your outstanding body guard.

Yours sincerely

Chastity

The Mid-Autumn Festival was on September 18th, and I was told that after this festival the cool weather would be coming, but it took a long time getting to Guangzhou. The Mid-Autumn Festival was interesting to observe. The lead-up to the festival reminded me a little of Western Christmas with lots of lantern decorations, huge fruit bowls and baskets for sale in the shops and also lovely moon cakes. I bought a pretty little lantern just to feel I was part of the celebration, and of course I made sure I had the wonderful fruit. I received a beautiful gift pack of assorted moon cakes from the school where I was teaching. The moon cakes were like marzipan with different fillings such as egg yolk, nuts, and fruit; it is a bit of "pot luck" as to what you find inside the moon cake. They are very nice but very fattening and filling. I must admit I ate only a few and gave the rest away.

The Mid-Autumn Festival dates back over 3,000 years to moon worshipping in the Shang Dynasty. Ancient Chinese emperors worshipped the moon in the autumn, as they believed that the practice would bring them another good harvest year.

The tradition of eating moon cakes during the festival began in the Yuan Dynasty. At the end of this dynasty (1271-1368, a dynasty ruled by the Mongols), the Han people's army wanted to overthrow the rule of the Mongols, and so they planned an uprising. One day, the military counselor of the Han People's Army, Liu Bowen, thought out a strategy related to moon cakes. He asked his soldiers to spread the rumour that there would be a serious disease in winter and eating moon cakes was the only way to cure the disease. He then asked his soldiers to write on pieces of paper, "Uprising, on the night of the Mid-Autumn Festival," and put them into moon cakes to sell to the common Han people. When the night of the Mid-Autumn Festival came, a huge uprising broke out. From then on, people eat moon cakes every Mid-Autumn Festival to commemorate the uprising.

和平

The Mid-Autumn Festival is also known as the festival for lovers because of the story about Chang E and Hou Yi. Folklore has it that, a long time ago, there were ten suns rising in the sky, which scorched all the crops and drove people into dire poverty.

A hero named Hou Yi was very worried about this; he went to the top of the Kunlun Mountain and, summoning up his superhuman strength, drew his extraordinary bow and shot down the nine superfluous suns one after the other. He also ordered the last sun to rise and set on time.

For this reason, he was respected and loved by the people and lots of people of high regard came to him to learn martial arts. One of these was named Peng Meng. Hou Yi had a beautiful and kind-hearted wife named Chang E. One day, on his way to the Kunlun Mountain to call on friends, he ran into the Empress of Heaven, Wangmu. She presented him with a parcel of elixir, which, it was said, would enable a person to be taken straight to heaven if they took it. Hou Yi, however, hated to be parted from his wife. So he gave the elixir to Chang E to keep safely for the time being. Chang E hid the parcel in a treasure box on her dressing table where, unexpectedly, it was seen by Peng Meng.

One day, when Hou Yi was out hunting with his followers, Peng Meng rushed into the bedroom with his sword in his hand and forced Chang E to hand over the elixir. Aware that she was unable to defeat Peng Meng, Chang E made a snap decision. She turned around and opened her treasure box, took out the elixir and swallowed it in one gulp. As soon as she swallowed it, her body floated off the ground, out the window and toward heaven. Peng Meng escaped.

When Hou Yi returned home at dark, he found out from the maidservants what had happened. Overcome with grief, Hou Yi looked up into the night sky and called out the name of his beloved wife. To his surprise, he found that the moon was especially clear and bright and on it there was a swaying shadow that looked exactly like his wife. He tried his best to chase after the moon. But as he ran, the moon retreated; as he withdrew, the moon came back. He could not get to the moon at all.

Thinking of his wife day and night, Hou Yi then had an incense table that Chang E loved arranged in the back garden. He put on the table sweetmeats and fresh fruits that Chang E enjoyed most, and held a memorial ceremony for her, as she was sentimentally attached to him in the palace of the moon.

和平

Just after the Mid-Autumn Festival in October, Nesupia arranged a cultural evening for all the teachers as well as all the Chinese TAs and office staff. A calligraphy teacher came to teach us Chinese calligraphy, which is a beautiful Chinese art but certainly is very difficult to master. Other Chinese girls taught us to play *mah-jong*. This is a very difficult game to learn but one which is very popular in China. On any evening on any street you can see groups of people sitting around a card table on the footpath playing *mah-jong*. The solitaire version is a free puzzle game based on a classic Chinese game for four people. *Mah-jong* is a very confusing game and one that I am sure I will never master. It was a wonderful evening with many new things about the Chinese culture to learn and continue to study if that was your wish.

7 A NEW CULTURE

A nation's culture resides in the hearts and in the soul of its people. – Mahatma Gandhi

The first week in October every year is the National Day holiday. Everyone in China has a week's holiday in celebration of October 1, 1949 when Chairman Mao declared the New China at Tiananmen Square in Beijing. It is called the Golden Week, as millions of people use that time to go shopping or travel to visit family and friends. I had an invitation to go to the seaside near Shenzhen with a group of teachers. But instead I arranged to undertake what proved to be an exciting trip with my Australian friend Tania. We called it our *Thelma and Louise* trip based on the movie of that name. A couple of my workmates from Brisbane had been transferred to work on a project in *Aotou*, a little fishing village two hours' bus ride east of Guangzhou. It was as far East as we could go without going into the China Sea. My ex workmates Roy and Mark from Brisbane were now living there and they invited me to visit. Having a week's holiday was a good opportunity to accept that invitation.

I was warned by everybody—teachers and the teachers' assistants—not to embark on the trip because no one had ever heard of the little fishing village or the closest big city called Hui Yang (196 km east of Guangzhou). We were to catch a bus from Guangzhou to Hui Yang and then a smaller bus or a taxi from Hui Yang to Aotou. Well, I took no notice of anyone, as I could not see what could be so difficult about the trip. My challenge was to buy a ticket at the bus station and to find out which station the bus left from (there are several huge bus stations in Guangzhou). I finally got the information from Elvis, Peter's TA, and I asked him to write in Chinese characters, "I wish to buy a ticket from Guangzhou to Hui Yang."

So, early in the morning, Tania and I embarked on our adventure which we had been warned about. We were very excited, as we felt we were so brave. We caught the local bus in Guangzhou to the huge bus station and easily found the place to buy the ticket. What we also found was a *long* queue; I have been told that long queues are normal at bus stations. Finally we were at the front of the queue and I handed over my little piece of paper with Chinese characters and received a piece of paper back with 75 RMB ($12.50) written on it so I knew what money to give the teller. With our tickets in hand we then had to go through the departure area (just like an airport) and find the gate which led to the bus. As all the writing was in Chinese characters we had no idea where to go, but we looked around and found a lady with a friendly face who was guarding one of the exits. After looking at our tickets she kindly escorted us to the correct bus.

It was a very comfortable, air-conditioned bus and we had a front seat, which was great as we had an excellent view. The bus trip out of Guangzhou was interesting, driving through suburbs which all began to look alike, the same streets, the same shops, the same people, the same traffic and finally we glimpsed the Chinese countryside which I had longed to see. How fascinating it was! The highway was super-modern six-laned with lovely landscaped gardens on either side and between the lanes. We were amazed at how clean and tidy it was. We drove through small banana plantations as well as fields with crops which we found hard to identify. We saw tiny shacks where we guessed the farming family lived. I had expected to see factories side by side but this was not the case. We followed the highway east that leads to Hong Kong for a little while until we turned off to go northeast. We saw a few factories and huge construction sites but were not able to ascertain exactly what they were. I was dying to ask someone a lot of questions but unfortunately my Chinese was not yet good enough. I was longing to learn more Chinese so I could communicate.

We heard a noise which we had not heard for a long time; the bus driver kept honking the horn. We couldn't work out why, and thought that perhaps he had a deprived childhood and had no toys to play with, so now the horn on the bus was his toy! We could only guess.

We arrived in Hui Yang to find a very busy little town, actually a very noisy town. I could not work out what the noise was; I did not remember this from Guangzhou. It was such a puzzle to me. I found out later that the noise was the honking of the horns in Hui Yang. In Guangzhou this is illegal and that is why the traffic seems so noisy in Hui Yang in comparison to Guangzhou. I found that very interesting. I often wondered why no one honked their horns in Guangzhou. I had many occasions when riding in a taxi where I would have done so if I was driving. But the taxi driver didn't; not even to warn a cyclist. They just stayed behind the cyclist until it was safe to pass.

We arrived at a small bus station with lots of taxis outside waiting for passengers. We had our pick of many, but really wanted to add to our adventure by catching the bus to Aotou. I had instructions from Roy where to catch the bus but it was not as easy to find as I had hoped and so I phoned Roy for help. He said the easiest way would be to catch a taxi to the Holiday Inn at Aotou. We had a choice of many taxis and we decided on one. As we got into the taxi I handed Roy's business card (in Chinese) to the driver. There was great confusion as we then realised that he didn't know where Aotou was. We panicked a little and wanted to get out of the taxi but the doors were locked. HELP! We waited anxiously for a few minutes as the taxi driver was "in conference" with other taxi drivers giving him advice. One taxi driver even tried to convince us to come with him! What a drama! Finally the taxi driver drove off and we were rather anxious to know if he actually had been given the correct advice. I keenly watched for signs that would indicate we were on the right track and soon I saw a sign indicating Aotou, then I felt okay.

和平

We arrived in Aotou to find almost nothing. I was told it was a fishing village but there were no fishing houses or even huts. What we found were two very new buildings, a Holiday Inn hotel and a large office building. We also found about twelve little shops, restaurants and bars built in a row. They looked as if they were new also.

Roy met us and treated us to a delightful lunch in one of the new restaurants, and I must say it was the best Chinese food I had eaten in China. Roy told me that people from the north of China owned the restaurant and it was "Northern food." I was led to believe that the Cantonese Food (from the Guangdong area) was the best Chinese food in China, but that has not been my experience so far.

We were told by Roy over lunch that all the buildings had developed when the Nickel Project had commenced in Aotou and before that there was nothing, as the fishing families live on their boats.

After lunch Roy showed us around the small "fishing village," which took three minutes! We saw pretty little fishing boats way out on the bay, but only a few, as most of the fishing boats were out fishing, of course. Roy told us that when the fishing boats come in to the little harbour at night several fishermen tie the fronts of their boats together to create a flat deck which becomes a little "village square" where the families gather at night to share their evening meals. I guess they also discuss the day's fishing events and tell the usual fishing stories "about the big one that got away." There was a little area at the back of the fishing boats where the family cooked, lived and slept. I would have loved to have stayed to see the "gathering of the fishing boats" in the evening but unfortunately we had to catch the last bus back to Guangzhou. I thought perhaps next time I could stay overnight at the Holiday Inn, which had a perfect view over the bay.

After our sightseeing, Tania and I had a lovely surprise at the Holiday Inn. Due to the fact there are about six-hundred expatriates from around the world in Aotou working on the project, the Holiday Inn set up a fantastic supermarket with all the Western food one could wish for. Tania and I really thought we had died and gone to heaven. We found Dutch Rye bread, Danish butter, Belgian chocolate, Paul Newman's tomato sauce for spaghetti, American popcorn, and, yes, I could go on and on.

We went mad shopping and spent almost 200 RMB, which is a fortune here but actually is only $34.

We enjoyed a lovely few hours with another of my ex-workmates from the Project. Mark and his family lived in their nice two-bedroom suite in the Holiday Inn Hotel overlooking the beautiful, peaceful bay. There were a few scattered fishing boats slowly making their way into the bay toward the end of the afternoon after their day of fishing.

Before catching the taxi back to Hui Yang, we checked out the local shops and found the most beautiful little clothing, gift and knick knack shop. There were so many beautiful and tasteful items, all hand-made, and I actually found a Danish cloth advent calendar made in the shape of a house with twenty-four little windows/pockets for the twenty-four little gifts. The calendar is a must for any Danish child, helping them to count the twenty-four days up to Christmas. It is probably popular with children all over the world who look forward to Christmas, especially from a Christian background. I just had to buy it, as it was beautifully handmade and only cost $6, which was unbelievable! There were many things I could have purchased but I was able to get out of the shop with only the Christmas calendar and a beautiful silk scarf for only $5. I was so proud of myself. I had so much willpower!

和平

The taxi ride back to the bus station in Hui Yang was uneventful and we arrived in plenty of time to catch the last bus back to Guangzhou at 6 p.m. We were able to purchase a ticket easily as one of Roy's Chinese work colleagues had written a message on a piece of paper in Chinese script.

Our trip back to Guangzhou was two and a half-hours. This was thirty minutes longer than the trip to Aotou due to heavy traffic as we got closer to Guangzhou. It was an interesting return trip, as we saw the same stretch of highway, villages and towns in the dark. How different the buildings looked all lit up by neon lights.

We were back in Guangzhou at 8:30 p.m. and were very happy with our little *Thelma and Louise* trip and very proud that we had done what many others seemed to think was impossible. As far as we were concerned, there was nothing impossible about it; it was just a wonderful adventure.

I wanted to make the most of my first holidays in China and planned to see as much as possible. Peter arranged for his TA, Elvis, and his friends to take us to a beautiful picturesque mountain area south of Guangzhou called Xiqiao Shan, which is a popular mountain for hiking by Chinese people. There is also a huge Buddha statue which is popular with the local Chinese. We caught a bus early in the morning and got off in a tiny village from where we had to walk up the mountain. There was a cable car but we decided to walk up, not realising how far it was. When we eventually got to the big Buddha statue we were exhausted. Then we had to climb another two-hundred or so steps to actually get up to the statue for a closer look. I was so exhausted I could hardly walk. Elvis lent me a hand and kept encouraging me by saying, "You will feel better when we get to the top." And he was right; I did feel better when I had finally reached the top of the steps. It was worth the climb seeing the huge Buddha up close and observing many people burning incense and praying in front of Buddha and making special requests.

We sat down on a bench and ate our lunch and very soon there was a crowd of Chinese people sitting in a circle around us observing this odd foreign couple, tall Peter and tiny me! It was amusing to feel like a fish in a fishbowl. Some little children were brave and came closer. I spoke slowly to one of the little boys saying, "Hello, how are you?" and he bravely said, "Fine, thank you" and then ran away screaming something in Chinese at the top of his voice!

Elvis told us the little boy said to his mother, "Mummy, Mummy, a foreigner just spoke to me, and I spoke back!" His mother responded by telling him how very clever he was. It is amazing how much enjoyment you can bring by being friendly and just saying a few words in English to a Chinese child.

Elvis decided we should all walk down the mountain a different way from the way we came up. He assured us it was very easy and a very picturesque walk. It was beautiful but it was very difficult, as we had to walk through caves and across streams. By the time we got to the bottom my feet were so sore and swollen I soaked them in a cooling stream to relieve the pain. To my amazement, several Chinese women seeing this thought it was a good idea and decided to do the same, sending me a "thumbs up" and a big smile while we sat there soaking our poor sore feet together. After a very exhausting day we were happy to get home and also very thankful for the adventure.

On another day of the holidays, I had made arrangements to do a sightseeing tour around Guangzhou, again with Peter, his TA Elvis and his girlfriend as our guides. It was great to have a guided tour of Guangzhou, especially because Elvis had studied up on all the sights he thought we should see. He was able to give us a lot of information about each sight we visited, like the beautiful Yuexiu Park and the memorial to Dr. Sun Yat-sen.

Catching the subway around the city was easy being guided by Elvis. He also took us to see the ancestral home of the Chen Clan family, which is now a museum. It was a most impressive building which gave us an insight into how a wealthy family lived one-hundred and fifty years ago in Guangzhou. It had an exquisite and spacious courtyard. The building was designed not only as an ancestral home and academy for a noble family, but also as a club for people from the same town to get together, something like a present-day Guangzhou representative office for a city. Shortly after its completion, the Chen Clan Academy began attracting people from various counties who had come to the provincial capital for business. They relaxed at the Academy, making friends, renewing friendships, looking for business opportunities as well as closing business deals.

和平

After the China National holiday, my exciting life continued. Teaching with Patty as a TA was easy and enjoyable but soon she had to move on to help a new young teacher. However, in the time she was with me, she trained another young girl to be my TA. Her name was Jean and she was a very clever young girl in her early twenties. She was from a large family of six children, from the seaport of Shantou in Eastern China. Jean was studying for her Economics degree in Guangzhou and wanted to work in an English environment to improve her language skills. Both her parents were doctors and they wanted to have many children so they kept paying the government the fine to have more children. For each child it became more and more expensive, so eventually after six children her father said that was enough. Jean was very wonderful young woman and we formed a very good working relationship and friendship which continues to this day. I still consider her one of my closest friends in China.

November and the Guangzhou autumn were upon us. After eight weeks of very hot, humid weather we had finally found some relief in the cooler Guangzhou autumn. We could actually now go for a walk for ten minutes and not become dripping wet from perspiration. I had been very lucky, as I had a fully air conditioned apartment and my classrooms were air-conditioned as well. Other teachers lived in apartments where only the bedrooms were air-conditioned and they taught in hot classrooms. Nice as it was, unfortunately, the cooler weather also gave me a bad cold which I found difficult to shake off. I refused to stay in bed and continued to teach every day. Some days I didn't have much voice and so Jean, my TA, had to do most of the talking; fortunately, her English was very good.

I would also play games like charades with the students where I would do body movements and facial expressions and they had to guess what I was trying to say. It was a lot of fun for the students and good practice for me to communicate without speaking.

While I shared the apartment with Peter at Fortuna Gardens I had become friendly with a single mother named Grace who lived in the apartment on the same floor as us. We met in the lift, chatted and became friends. One day she invited me to her apartment for dinner. I asked her if I could bring my friend Peter and she agreed. After that first meeting, Peter and Grace continued their friendship which, after a couple of years, ended up in marriage and a baby girl.

My friendship with the Canadian teacher Betty developed, and one day in late November she asked me if I wanted to move into her apartment, which was in the other apartment block where Nesupia had rented apartments for the teachers. I gratefully accepted. Peter was leaving Nesupia after the first semester to work for another school and I wouldn't know who Nesupia would move in to share my apartment (two teachers always shared a two-bedroom apartment). Betty's apartment was much bigger than the one I shared with Peter and it was in the apartment block where most of the teachers lived on two floors. In the other apartment building the teachers lived on different floors and so there was not much contact among the teachers. In Betty's apartment block there was a lot of activity and fun among the teachers, as they lived so close together. I was excited about the idea and, after getting permission from the Nesupia office, we arranged a moving day in early December.

I knew it would be great to live with Betty. She had created a "home," as she had lived in Guangzhou and worked for Nesupia for five years. She had everything electrical and bookcases full of books; she was a bookworm. One concern was that Betty had not shared her apartment with another teacher before so she wasn't really sure how she would like it. But she was prepared to try.

Jenny lived in an apartment close to Betty's on a floor below, and I knew it would be nice to be close to Jenny as well. Jenny had been so wonderful to me; she lent me a lovely sleeping bag which I could use as a doona, and also a heater and a "dune jacket." This was a great help, as these were things I didn't need to buy as the cooler weather arrived.

The moving weekend went so well. I am a good packer and I had thirty-five neatly packed bags and suitcases. I was amazed how much I had collected in just three and a half months!

My friend Tania from the *Thelma and Louise* trip came to help me move, as well as Betty and Jenny. We met at Starbucks near The Garden Hotel (the only Starbucks coffee shop in Guangzhou at the time) for coffee to celebrate the move, and then we caught a taxi to my apartment at Fortuna Gardens. Peter and Larry were waiting for us to help move also. We carried the bags and suitcases downstairs in an assembly line and into two taxis. A short ride of 10 minutes brought us to my new apartment building. We then took all the bags up to the 5th floor of my new apartment (by lift, of course) and put them all in my room, which was much bigger than my bedroom at Fortuna Gardens. I then invited all 'the helpers' for lunch and Jenny decided we should go to a great Mongolian restaurant to have "chicken hot pot," which was chicken and vegetables on a bed of freshly made noodles with wonderful spices. The dish was placed in the middle of the table and everyone just picked up the food with chopsticks from the *huge* flat dish. It was so delicious. We also each had a lamb burger, which is lamb on flat bread with wonderful spices and it is absolutely scrumptious. It all only cost me 80 RMB ($13.50) for six people. I do prefer not to eat meat but sometimes to have a different eating experience I do eat a little meat.

The move only took the morning and then a couple of hours for lunch. In the afternoon I had to teach in the kindergarten and came home at 6 p.m. I spent Saturday evening unpacking and finding a place for everything and finished before I went to bed. I had to go and buy two sets of drawers to help me keep everything neat and tidy. At the supermarket just across the road I could buy some plastic sets of drawers, which were very handy. I was pleased with the end result.

On Sunday morning we went to church and it was so nice to be able to share that experience with

Betty. After church I spent the afternoon settling into the kitchen. The bathroom was nice with a great walk-in shower. We had no usable balcony—there was only a little balcony which was used as a laundry and drying area for our clothes.

I was happy with the view, and I had a pleasant surprise when I looked out the window and saw a lovely view of the square where a group of women were practising their fan dance on the Sunday afternoon. We also heard singers practising lovely old Chinese songs. Chinese people love to sing and dance. I woke up most mornings to the sound of Chinese chatting and lovely music and I felt so good; I was sure I was going to be so much happier there.

The living room was huge with lovely furniture and two *rocking chairs*! Betty and I were like two little old ladies sitting in our rocking chairs reading our Bible! There was a lovely dining room suite as well, which would be good for our Danish Christmas dinner I was going to host all my friends. Unfortunately, we could not have our Christmas until December 27th, as we were all teaching on Christmas Day. China, of course, doesn't celebrate Christmas and the Nesupia Company would not agree to give teachers a day off even though many teachers had asked for it. So we were all teaching our normal classes on Christmas Day. However, we decided we were all just going to have a Christmas party with the students and teach them about Christmas and we would make it a fun day.

8 FIRST CHRISTMAS AND NEW YEAR IN CHINA

Christmas ... is not an external event at all, but a piece of one's home that one carries in one's heart. – Freya Stark

During the month of December, we organised a Sunday evening Bible study group with Betty, Jenny, Larry, Trudee, John and me. It was very pleasant sitting in our living room reading the Bible and discussing meanings. Of course, every Sunday morning we would also go to the non-denominational church in a conference room in the Star Hotel. After having been closed down by the Chinese government a couple of month earlier the Church had reopened to the delight of all the church goers from around the world who would meet every Sunday morning to worship together. The reason why the government had approved the licence for the church to continue I never really understood. T.I.C. This is China

I had some sad news in December and that was that John and Trudee had decided to leave and return to Australia. They felt it was time to go home to their family. They missed their grandchildren and I could understand that.

As from mid-October, I was surprised to see there was so much to do with Christmas in China. All the big department stores and supermarkets played English Christmas carols and had so many Christmas decorations that it was almost like being home in Brisbane. It certainly was a pleasant surprise. Of course the majority of Christmas decorations are made in China and exported to other Christian countries, so it was no wonder they were making use of them in China as well!

In early December, I was shopping in Vanguard, the big supermarket across the road from where I lived, and lovely Christmas songs were being piped throughout the supermarket. Suddenly I got so emotional and stood there in the middle of the supermarket crying. I missed my daughter and the memories associated with Christmas and family.

During the month of December I told the students stories about Santa Claus and not about Jesus, as I had been told we were not allowed to talk to the students about religion. Nesupia organised a Christmas party with all the students on December 20th. It was an all day party we dubbed "Christmas in the park" with lots of games and gifts and sweets for the students. Each teacher and TA was responsible for setting up and organising games and all the games took place in a circle on a big football field. The students, led by a TA, could go from game to game and after each game get lollies. It was a big success and fortunately it was a sunny day, but as it was December it was cold. After the Christmas party, Nesupia took all the teachers to a restaurant for their Christmas party. It was a huge Chinese restaurant and the Chinese food that was served was delicious.

For Christmas Eve, I had received an invitation from the parents of one of my favourite Grade 1 students, Selina, to join them for dinner in a very large and expensive restaurant. I had met her parents at an open class for the students. Selina and her parents, Eddie and Helen, had lived in New

Zealand for four years and they both spoke English very well. Helen picked me up outside my apartment and we drove to the restaurant. I was looking forward to seeing Selina's little sister Grace, but she didn't come to the dinner. We went to a huge seafood restaurant and as we walked into the restaurant it seemed as if everyone was looking at us. Selina said, "Everyone is looking at us because we are with you. They all envy us because we have a foreign friend." It was so nice to hear a little girl say those words. Of course I would learn in the years to come that most foreigners received a lot of attention in China. We met Eddie at the restaurant and had a lovely dinner together with pleasant conversation. I gave Selina and Grace a Christmas stocking with little Christmas gifts inside and told Selina the story about the Christmas stocking and the first Saint Nicholas in Turkey. Selina took the christmas stocking home to Grace later. After dinner, Eddie drove me back to my apartment.

I felt so spoilt and privileged to have so many wonderful experiences just because I was a foreigner.

I enjoyed my first December in Guangzhou, with all the new and exciting experiences. Christmas was certainly in the air. I placed my Advent wreath on a table with four candles, one for each Sunday in Advent. I enjoyed lighting a candle each Sunday evening as is the custom in Denmark. I also had my Christmas Advent calendar which I had bought in the fishing village Aotou a few weeks earlier and my Christmas stocking had been hung up eagerly waiting for Santa to fill it (I could but hope!).

All the teachers had to teach normal hours on December 25th but I made sure Christmas Day was a lovely day spent in the classroom. On that day Jean, my TA, and I played games with the students and sang Christmas songs. I had also prepared Christmas cards and a Christmas gift for each student, which was accepted with joy. Jean and I played a trick on the students. Before giving them the Christmas gift I told them that Santa Claus would bring the gifts. Jean had hidden the gifts outside the classroom in a large red bag.

I told the students that Santa would fly through the sky in his sleigh pulled by nine reindeer and would land in the school yard. He would phone me as he was arriving, and if we looked out the window perhaps we would see him and his reindeer. I had arranged with Jean to phone me on my mobile phone without the students seeing her doing it, so when the phone rang I answered it and got very excited and told the students it was Santa Claus and he was arriving and if they looked out the window they may see him. As the students rushed to the window Jean went outside the classroom door and called out, "Look! Santa left some Christmas gifts."

The students got so excited. But they asked, "Where is Santa?" I told them that Santa was very busy and he had to fly off very quickly to give Christmas gifts to other children. They accepted that explanation, as their eyes were on the large red bag with Christmas gifts. I then asked them to sit down and I played a game with the students to teach them spelling. I said Santa Claus had written each student's name on the gift and as I picked up each gift I just said the first letter of the name and the students then had to guess who the gift was for. The distribution of each gift was met with huge applause from the students. After all the gifts had been handed out, I looked out the window and, to my surprise I saw a red Santa hat hanging in a tree outside. I told the students it was Santa's hat and that he must have lost it as he flew away. They believed me. A lovely day was had by one and all. I enjoyed it as much as the students.

A friend of Betty's was coming down from Beijing for Christmas and would be cooking us a traditional Canadian Christmas dinner on the 25th in the evening. The meal was delicious; turkey with cranberry sauce and vegetables.

On Boxing Day, the day after Christmas, all our friends gathered in our apartment and shared Christmas gifts. Then we all went out to a lovely restaurant situated on a beautiful lake to enjoy a dim sum lunch.

On December 27th I decided I would cook everyone a Danish Christmas dinner: roast pork with red cabbage, caramelised potatoes and rice pudding; in Danish it is called Ris-a-la-mande. I enjoyed cooking and preparing the Christmas meal from my country of birth. Even though I had lived in Australia for thirty-four years I had never given up the Danish Christmas traditions.

As China is not a Christian country, the days between Christmas and New Year were just normal working days, and New Year's Eve was not celebrated in China except by the young people who love to copy Western traditions. On New Year's Eve I had been asked to go to Sha Wan Kindergarten in Panyu to be part of a school play where the students would show their parents what they had learnt. There was singing and dancing by the students and my part was an English play which I had been rehearsing with the students. It was a delightful evening and it was rather strange to be in a huge room with about one thousand people and being the only Western person. Over the next many years I would learn to get used to that. Ms. Wang also attended the presentation and she kindly drove me home afterwards after treating me to dinner at a lovely seafood restaurant in Panyu.

I arrived home close to midnight and decided to walk to the Guangzhou Times Square (yes, Guangzhou also has a Times Square!) to see if there was any excitement at midnight. When I arrived there, I was met by a sea of young people just walking around or standing around near the big clock. It was very pleasant to mingle with the crowd, as many young people thought it was fun to say "Happy New Year" to me in English. Midnight came and nothing happened. There were no fireworks, as that is forbidden in Guangzhou. It is amazing, that in the country where fireworks were invented and are made for the rest of the world, but in the third largest city in China it is forbidden. Of course that is because of the danger connected to the fireworks. However organised fireworks is allowed and huge crowds of people go to special locations to watch fireworks on festivals such as Chinese New Year. I wandered home through the

New Year's streets feeling happy I was at least part of *something* on my first New Year in China.

In early January Betty asked me to move out of the apartment, as she found she didn't like sharing her apartment. I was sad but on the other hand I was going to be moved to the best apartment Nesupia had: a big three-bedroom apartment with a huge living room and a floor-to-ceiling window with a wonderful view. My bedroom was lovely. It had a beautiful window with a window seat and a great view. The new apartment was just down the hall and so it only took me thirty minutes to move the bits and pieces I had already collected in the four months I had been in China. I loved the new apartment. I would be sharing it with another teacher for a week but after that it was mine to be enjoyed all by myself.

和平

January 2004 was a cold month. Winter had certainly come to Guangzhou. We had moved straight from Christmas to Chinese New Year preparations. On December 27th, all the shops had changed their decorations and sales promotions from Western Christmas to Chinese New Year. The large shops must have had thousands of workers who worked overnight changing the decorations.

Jenny, who is excellent at looking after new teachers, introduced us to many types of lovely restaurants in the city such as vegetarian, Mongolian hot pot, Japanese and Vietnamese, to name just a few. Guangzhou is a trading city and people come from all over the world for Trade Fairs twice a year, and so there is a wide selection of restaurants from which to choose.

Jenny also introduced me to the "fabrics market," which is a huge shopping area with just fabrics and accessories. Many foreigners who come here have their clothes tailor-made because usually they are larger than Chinese people and find it difficult to buy clothes in shops. Many Canadian and American girls have their shorts and slacks made to fit. I did not have that problem, being 150 cm tall, and can easily fit into Chinese size clothes but Jenny convinced me to have a dress made, so I picked out the material and the tailor took my measurements and told me I could pick up the dress a few days later. When I picked up the dress, it didn't fit at all; it was very tight. I still had to pay for the dress, but I never wore it and eventually threw it out and decided having tailor-made clothes was not for me.

Jenny often phoned me to ask if I wanted to come and "hang out" or do some exciting things with her. She is the type of person who doesn't like to be alone. Often she would ask me to join her in a visit to a hair salon next to our apartment building to have our hair washed. Now this is a lot more exciting than it sounds! For as little as 10 RMB ($1.70) you could have your hair washed—not once but three times and conditioned. The hairdresser would take at least thirty minutes to wash and condition your hair, and then give you a full head, neck, arm, shoulder and facial massage. Then you get a full-body massage (with your clothes on) back, spine and legs (front and back). After that they blow-dry your hair to perfection. If you want to have your hair cut it is 20 RMB ($3.40). A few days before Chinese New Year, Jenny and I, along with four other teachers, went to the small hairdressing salon to have our hair washed and a massage and the staff got so excited when they saw us. That was good business for them. As a New Year's gift to us all, Jenny paid for us. She was always *very* generous.

I have lost count of all she gave me such as clothes, sleeping bags, household items and so on. I am in debt to her for the rest of my life. She told me one day she looked upon me as her mother in China.

She liked looking after her mother back home and now she said she had a mother to look after in China as well.

The month of January was also when I finally bought a mobile phone. As mobile phones were not so common in 2004 I thought I didn't need one. However I had a communication breakdown with my Saturday TA. My understanding was we should meet at the bus station to catch the bus to Panyu kindergarten at 7 a.m. on Saturday morning. My TA, Kerry, had understood we should meet at the Nesupia office. So there we were waiting for each other at different locations. I couldn't contact her and she couldn't contact me. Finally she realised we were meeting at the bus station and came. I realised that I needed a mobile phone in case of situations like that. So with the help of Jean, my TA at my main school, I purchased a cheap mobile phone. It was to make my life so much easier and pleasant for me as I was able to keep in touch with friends easily.

As I missed keeping in touch with Elizabeth, I also asked her to buy me an Australian mobile phone and SIM card with global roaming so we could keep in touch easily by text message. I felt like a new person having all this technology to make my life more enjoyable.

In January I also made friends with the parents of another one of my students, Craig. His father, Cai, was a lawyer and his mother was an accountant. They invited me out for dinner at the most wonderful restaurant. Being seen with a white person seemed to be "prestigious," and also being in the company of a teacher is a great honour. I didn't feel I was being used by these generous Chinese friends. I felt they appreciated me teaching their children and wanted to show their appreciation directly. Teachers are very highly regarded in China. Cai told me that teaching is the most respected profession in China, more than law or accountancy. I knew it wasn't always like that as I had read books about the Cultural Revolution like *Wild Swans* and during the Cultural Revolution the teaching profession was severely persecuted.

The weeks before Chinese New Year is a shopper's paradise in China: streets and stores are filled with sweets, nuts and many other foods as well as the "Chinese New Year tree." This is either a tree or a bush with dark green leaves with many mandarin oranges. There are thousands, or rather millions, of them sold on every corner and along every busy street. The tree brings luck for the following year, and so everyone must have one. There are real mandarin oranges on the tree but they are only for display. There are also the lovely peach tree branches. The branches have been cut off, and only a few flowers have sprung, but there are hundreds of little buds which will bloom during the festive season when the branch is placed indoors. That tree is supposed to keep away evil spirits, so this is another "must have"! Flowers are plentiful both in pots and as cut flowers. The traditional New Year flowers are chrysanthemums in different colours including yellow, white and orange and also the red Christmas star flower.

Chinese New Year shopping is very frantic. Traffic comes to a halt, as there are so many people and cars. Thousands of delivery riders tie the mandarin orange trees or peach tree branches to the back of their delivery bike and easily weave their way through the traffic with this very heavy load. It has to be seen to be believed!

Jenny and Larry invited me to come to Tianjin, the harbour city of Beijing, for Chinese New Year, which would be on January 22nd that year. Larry's parents and grandmother lived there. Larry told me the sad remarkable story of his family since the Cultural Revolution in China from 1966 to 1976 affected his family greatly. His grandparents had been wealthy silk merchants before 1949 when the

PRC (People's Republic of China) was established on October 1, 1949. All their wealth was confiscated by the new government. They lost everything. Their huge mansion in Tianjin was taken away from them and divided into small apartments. Larry's grandparents only kept a small room which served as living room, dining room and bedroom, and they also had a very small kitchen with only a coal stove.

Larry's parents were both university professors and between 1966 and 1976 they were sacked from their university positions. They were then sent to Mongolia to a tiny village to work as teachers and to do hard labour in the fields. As Larry was only a baby, his parents left him behind in Tianjin with his grandparents and Larry didn't get to know his parents until he was fifteen years old. He was brought up with his grandparents in their tiny apartment. Eventually, after the death of Chairman Mao in 1976, his parents returned from Mongolia and took up their positions at the university again.

I had been invited to celebrate Chinese New Year with the family, which was very exciting. As the months of January and February are very cold in the north, I needed to buy some warm winter clothes. Jenny knew the best shopping areas in Guangzhou where you could get a bargain, and so she helped me buy a wonderful warm, padded, ankle-length coat with a fur-lined hood which would keep me very warm in the minus 15 degrees in Tianjin and Beijing. I only paid 300 RMB for the coat which is equal to $50. The coat would have cost at least $500 in Australia.

We would be travelling by train from Guangzhou to Beijing and from there to Tianjin; it would be a train trip of about thirty-six to forty hours. This was to be my first experience of travelling during Chinese New year and indeed travelling on a Chinese train up through this huge country.

Train tickets could only be purchased by lining up and waiting your turn to buy the ticket at the train station, and only a certain number of tickets were sold every day. Larry would get up early every morning to go to the train station to line up but only on the fifth day was he able to buy the tickets. At that time there were no more tickets left for January 17th, which was the day we wanted to travel; he could only get tickets for January 22nd being the day *after* Chinese New Year. He didn't have a choice, and so it meant that we would not be in Tianjin to celebrate the New Year with his family.

Chinese New Year is the biggest festival in China and millions of people travel home to be with their families. The Chinese system cannot cope with that number of people travelling at the same time, and so many miss out. A lot of people buy "standing tickets" and stand up on the train for long distances.

I was all packed on January 22nd and ready for Beijing. I was only taking three sets of warm clothes and three sets of thermal underwear and thermal socks. I would see what the weather was like in the cold North. If I needed to buy boots that were warmer and more waterproof than the ones I had, I would buy them in Beijing or Tianjin. We were also taking food for the train, as the food on the train was very expensive.

It was going to be so exciting. We would leave Guangzhou at 10 a.m. and arrive in Beijing late on January 23rd, as it took well over thirty-six hours. It was a train trip of about 2,300 km. We would then hire a minibus to take everyone to Jenny and Larry's apartment and in due course would go to Larry's parents' home.

I had decided I would make this trip a time for learning as much Mandarin as possible from Larry's parents, as they were well-educated, I would be learning perfect Mandarin. What an opportunity!

On January 22nd, we made our way to the train station to board the train for Beijing. Wearing warm clothes and the thick padded coat, I felt I was ready for the cold north. We had booked a "soft sleeper," which was a very comfortable way of travelling. There were four bunks in each compartment, and as we were first in the compartment, Jenny and I took the two lower bunks and Larry an upper bunk. We were very fortunate on the whole journey that we only had one other person in the compartment for a short distance. A few of the other teachers were also travelling north to Beijing and I realised, by visiting them in other areas of the train, how lucky I was to have a soft bed compartment. As they didn't have a lot of money, they travelled in "hard sleepers," which was an open compartment with six bunks crammed into each compartment. Of course, they were young people so they could cope with the discomfort. The most unpleasant area of the train was the seating area. I couldn't imagine sitting up for thirty-six hours. I walked through the area and the people looked very uncomfortable. I was told that many poor people who have very little money would buy standing tickets and stand up for the thirty-six to forty hours or sit on the floor of the train. There was also an eating car where we spent time sitting, chatting, eating and drinking.

Mostly, I spent the time in the compartment looking out the window, making notes of things I wanted to remember, especially noticing the landscape and the tiny villages we drove through. China is a huge country with magnificent scenery, but what I was missing was the picturesque villages like you see in Europe and Scandinavia. In China, all the villages are brown and grey and the only colour was the red Chinese New Year banners people hang around the doors for health and wealth in the coming year. Of course, the red Chinese flag was seen flying from flagpoles and buildings everywhere, adding colour to the otherwise grey landscape.

As we were travelling further north, away from Guangzhou province, we could see how the climate changed from mild in the south with trees still clad in their leaves to a colder winter where the trees had bare branches. It was a magnificent sight to see the birds' nests on the bare branches. As we were nearing the large cities, I saw what looked like colourful material in the trees. It looked so pretty with many blue, green, orange, red and yellow colours. I was fascinated. What was it? I soon realised that it was plastic bags which had blown away from the rubbish dump near the city and I didn't consider it "pretty" anymore! China has a huge pollution problem with plastic bags and Styrofoam. I know the government is working on reducing pollution but controlling 1.3 billion people is not an easy task. It will take time.

I enjoyed following the route of the train up through China on a large map (I love maps). Through the different provinces I marked on my map the cities we passed through and where we stopped. When the train stopped we could see hundreds of vendors on the platforms with carts of food for the travellers to buy. As food is often very expensive on trains, many travellers choose to bring their food or buy at the stops. As we were getting further and further north the weather got colder and colder and the vendors would appear bigger and bigger as they would wear more and more clothes!

Larry's brother was there to greet us as we arrived at the main station at Tianjin. As we stepped off the train I thought I would die as a freezing breeze hit my face, it was like being pricked with a thousand needles at the same time. I couldn't believe how cold it was. I had to cover my face completely with scarves except for a small slit to look through. It brought back memories of my cold winters in

Denmark as a child, and I remembered why I wanted to leave Denmark to go and live in sunny Northern Australia.

Larry's brother had hired a minivan to drive Jenny, Larry and me, together with the five other teachers travelling with us, to a little village called Dagang one hour by car East of Tianjin. There were nine people to get into the tiny minivan with a lot of luggage. The last person to fit into the van was Larry, and he actually had to lie across the three people on the second row of seats! It was a very cramped but fun trip from Tianjin to Dagang, a little university city outside Tianjin where Larry's parents lived. Jenny and Larry also had an apartment there, which they used only once a year when they went to Dagang.

I learnt that Tianjin is the fifth largest city in China with a population of about eight to nine million people. Wuhan is the fourth largest city. Guangzhou is the third largest city with about nine million people (fifteen million people if you add the surrounding areas), and Beijing is the second largest (sixteen million) with Shanghai being the largest with eighteen million (at the time of writing).

Tianjin is Beijing's port city and has a very strong European flavour. I had to remind myself I was in China, as this city looked so European. In 1858, the British persuaded China, with the help of gunboats I might add, to open up Tianjin to foreign trading. The rest of Europe soon joined the British. Most European countries had left their mark on this now huge port city.

Tianjin and Dagang were two of the cities used during the 2008 Olympics; several sporting events were held there. Dagang is a city of some 30,000 people, a very pretty little "village" by Chinese standards even though it was dressed in its winter grey. I thought it was pretty because all the villages I had seen travelling up through China had gray and brown building but the buildings in Dagang were white. Larry's father was a Professor of Chinese languages and scripts and his mother Professor of Science at the university at Dagang. They were both brilliant scholars.

Larry's parents welcomed us with open arms. We met them outside a large restaurant where they had booked a private room for all the foreign guests and Larry's brother, wife and niece who also joined the party.

No expense was spared and the hospitality knew no bounds from the generous hosts. There was lots of laughter and *gan bai* (cheers) were heard throughout the evening with Australians, Americans and Canadians making friends with the northern Chinese Han people.

Over the next two weeks I was so fortunate to experience again and again the wonderful hospitality of those kind people. We had a noodle and *jiao zi* evening where Larry's father taught me to make homemade noodles the old fashioned way, just by slicing the homemade dough (similar to bread dough) into a pot of boiling water and out came the most delicious homemade noodles. A traditional northern China food is *jiao zi*, which is a kind of dumpling with a filling of vegetable or meat. You take a small pancake, then place the filling in the middle and fold it over so the filling is secure inside. The folding must be done a certain way and it must look pretty. I never managed to make mine look pretty. After that, the *jiao zi* is than placed in a pot of boiling water until cooked; sometimes, after the boiling, the *jiao zi* is also fried which makes a delicious snack or part of a meal. It was a wonderful family dinner with lots of singing and taking photos. I was encouraged to sing a Chinese love song which I had been practising ever since I arrived in China called *Ni wen wo ai*. It is a Chinese love song translated into English as *The Moon Represents my Heart*. It was my first attempt at singing the song for others and it was immortalised by Larry's brother on his video camera!

We left the lovely little village of Dagang to make a trip to Tianjin to visit Larry's eighty-eight-year-old grandmother who had brought him up. Her husband had died but she still lived in the one tiny room with a very small kitchen with a coal burner that had been allocated to her by the government in 1949 when they confiscated the beautiful mansion she shared with her husband. How sad it was so see this dignified old Chinese lady living such a humble life. The small room was used as a dining, living and also bedroom. To go to bed she had to collapse the dining room table to make space for the bed. We spent a few hours in her tiny abode and I wished I had been able to speak Mandarin so I could have spoken to her, but all we could do was to look at each other, smile and hold hands. I hoped she could feel I was an admirer of her dignity and courage.

9 BEIJING ADVENTURES

I wandered everywhere, through cities and countries wide. And everywhere I went, the world was on my side. – Roman Payne

From Tianjin we continued by train to Beijing to see the famous sights. In Beijing we stayed in a very nice hostel in the "nightlife area," which was where Larry wanted to stay. I would have preferred to stay close to the centre of the city.

When in Beijing it is a *must* to visit Tiananmen Square, which means "Gate of Heavenly Peace." It is the largest square in the world and at first sight it is overwhelming. The square covers 40.5 hectares and one can't help but reflect on the terrible day on June 4, 1989 when Chinese soldiers and tanks opened fire on the student demonstrators. Looking at the peaceful square today it is difficult to visualise what a horrible and tragic event that was. At one end of Tiananmen Square is a huge monument which is said to hold Chairman Mao's body, which may or may not be the real body … who knows? I wanted to see it but was told I had to queue up at 6 a.m. and there would be a strong possibility I would not get in anyway. It is a very popular tourist site for Chinese people, with only a certain number of people being allowed in each day, and so I decided not to waste my time. It was also amazing to see the huge building of The Great Hall of the People, which I have heard so much about.

A visit to The Forbidden City is also a must when you go to Beijing and to have a photo taken in front of Chairman Mao's huge picture. The photo cannot be missed as it is hang at the entrance to The Forbidden City. As they say, "When in Rome, do as the Romans do." I also had my photo taken so many times by Chinese tourists. "Can we have a photo with you?" they said, not in so many words, of course, but by sign language. I have no idea why they would want a group photo with me in it! What do they tell their friends and family when they show them the photo? Something like, "She is my friend," or "This is a funny-looking long-nosed foreigner we thought it would be fun to have in our photo!" Who knows? They went away happy and I felt I had done a good deed. I hate to think what I looked like in the photos all wrapped up against the cold weather. I wore my huge, ankle-length, warm padded coat and a new pair of Russian boots I had purchased. They were warm as toast being lined with lamb's wool. After I was dressed in my warm clothes I didn't mind going outside, as I felt so warm and cosy. But I must have looked like a snowman.

I spent almost a whole day looking through The Forbidden City. Like most other tourists, I marvelled at the magnificent structures and the grandness of it all, trying to imagine the emperors living here for hundreds of years hidden from their subjects and especially the last emperor Pu Yi, who spent several years as a prisoner in his own palace.

Larry, Jenny and I made arrangements to join a one day tour to The Great Wall. Seeing The Great Wall was something I had dreamed of for a long time and after a pleasant one-hour drive north of Beijing in a minivan, I caught the first glimpse of the magnificent structure and my heart skipped a beat. It brought tears to my eyes; I am not really sure why. It was just so wonderful to see the famous sights, and it was all and much more than I had imagined and expected.

The Great Wall was started over two thousand years ago and additional sections of the wall were added over the next fifteen hundred years. The Great Wall is one of the largest construction projects ever completed. It's a series of fortifications made of stone, brick, wood and other materials built across the historical northern borders to ward off invaders.

It was an awesome experience to walk on The Great Wall on stones where soldiers had walked for two thousand years guarding their homeland from the barbarians from the north. No words could describe the magnitude of this, "the greatest man-made construction ever."

There is a big debate about exactly how long the Great Wall is. It is difficult to estimate, as there are many different sections of the wall. However, it has been written that the length from the East coast line of China toward the Western frontier is 8,850 km (5,550 miles). But in 1987 the wall was measured and, adding all the different parts of The Great Wall together, the total length is about 21,196 km.

Jenny introduced me to an amazing "Peking duck" restaurant near Tiananmen Square. It was rather famous, judging by photos of famous people on the walls who had dined there, such as presidents and vice-presidents from several countries, famous actors and singers. It was my first taste of Peking duck and I fell in love with it, and in fact every day after my first introduction I went back alone and had a serving of Peking duck all by myself. It is Beijing's most famous dish and it is called Peking duck as Peking is the previous name of Beijing. Peking duck is traditionally served with Mandarin pancakes and green onions for brushing on the hoisin sauce. As I was sitting eating my delicious Peking duck I couldn't help but wonder where Al Gore and the Greek pianist Yanni were sitting when they dined here.

Jenny wanted to meet up with an old Canadian friend in Beijing and they arranged to meet at an Irish pub near our hostel. It was a typical Irish pub; you would be forgiven for thinking you were in Ireland, not in Beijing. We were a large group of expatriate Australians and Canadians enjoying a night out and I actually decided to have a Carlsberg beer, a beer from my home country Denmark. Even though I don't usually drink beer, I must say I enjoyed it. I even had a photo taken to send to my daughter so she could see her mother drinking a beer!

During my time in Beijing I was enjoying feeling young and free. I met many people from different countries who I befriended and spend time talking to. I enjoy making new friends when I travel. I feel everyone has a story and I like to hear it.

After our wonderful time in Beijing we returned by train to Tianjin and then by taxi to Dagang for a few days before returning to Guangzhou. The short train trip was pleasant but on arrival at Tianjin train station it was a challenge to find a taxi. Fortunately, Larry being Chinese and knowing the culture did lots of negotiation with taxi drivers but most of them would not take us to Dagang or they charged a huge amount of money, which Larry was not prepared to pay. Finally he negotiated a reasonable price with one taxi driver and we loaded our luggage into the boot of the taxi and drove toward Dagang. Jenny and I sat in the back and Larry sat in the front, which was rather unusual as in Beijing there is a rule that no one can sit in the front of a taxi for security reasons. There is a steel mesh between the driver's seat and the back seat for security reasons as well.

As we were driving along we listened to the conversation between Larry and the taxi driver and we noticed it got louder and louder. Their voices were getting angrier and eventually the taxi driver stopped and they continued to argue. Jenny had lived in China for three years and spoke Chinese rather well but she could not understand what they were saying, as they spoke so quickly. We tried to ask Larry what the problem was but he was too busy arguing to answer us. Eventually, we found out that the taxi driver had changed his mind and wanted twice the amount of money he had originally quoted.

After a long time Jenny decided that she didn't want to listen to the arguing anymore and told me that we had to get out of the taxi but not without our luggage. She asked the taxi driver to open the boot so we could get the luggage but he refused. He said if we didn't pay the amount he asked he would take our luggage. Jenny then got the bright idea of pulling the back seat forward and then somehow getting to the luggage in the boot from the back seat. We quickly pulled all our luggage out and threw it on to the grassy area next to the road and jumped out of the taxi.

However, Larry didn't want to give up. He demanded that the taxi driver take us to Dagang for the price he had first quoted at Tianjin railway station. Eventually, Jenny got Larry out of the taxi and the taxi driver drove off very angry, as Larry had refused to pay him any money. And so there we were left on the side of a country road which seemed deserted. There were no houses nearby and we didn't know how we were going to get to Dagang. We waited on the side of the road for a long time and to our relief, we were able to wave down an old bus that came along. The bus was completely full but we somehow managed to squeeze in with our luggage and arrived in Dagang in the late afternoon. I was so relieved but I felt lucky I had Jenny as support.

After two weeks up in the cold north we once again boarded the train and had a very relaxed and comfortable train trip in a "soft-sleeper compartment" back to Guangzhou. It was interesting to travel from the cold north back toward the warmer climate in the south of China. The bare trees would be replaced with trees dressed in their beautiful leaves and as we moved closer toward Guangdong province, the people we saw on the train stations as we drove through would be wearing fewer clothes.

I was amazed how happy I felt being back in Guangzhou, even though I had only lived there six months; it was like coming home.

It was strange walking into my apartment, as there were changes. There were suitcases and things everywhere. I was soon to find out that while I was away a couple had moved into my apartment: an older (forty-something) Canadian man Garry and his very young (twenty-something) English girlfriend Ada. It was a surprise to me, but I welcomed them and we spent some time chatting before I unpacked my suitcase.

10 TEACHING PLEASURES

Strive not to be a success, but rather to be of value. – Albert Einstein

I was very happy being back in Guangzhou and I was glad to find out that I had the same teaching schedule and the same TA, Jean, as the previous semester. I would see all my students from last semester again.

As a welcome back to the new semester, Nesupia took us all out for lunch at a lovely Chinese Restaurant. Every time I looked at some food which was unrecognisable, I asked the Chinese girls at the table what it was and the answer was usually, "If you taste it you will find out." Not really good enough for me!

I was glad to be back at work; I liked being in a routine and couldn't wait to see the students the first day of school. It was still very cold in Guangzhou and so I continued to wear the same clothes I wore in Beijing. Yes, wearing my Russian boots lined with lamb's wool! I wanted to keep warm so I didn't get the flu. I got over my slight cold I had in Beijing and didn't want it to come back.

It was an interesting experience sharing the apartment with my new flatmates, Ada and Gerry. I didn't see them much because during the week I was teaching every day, and Saturday and Sunday I went out if I wasn't teaching.

After a few weeks they moved to another apartment and I then shared the apartment with a Canadian (Native Indian) teacher for a couple of weeks. She could not accept the teaching methods Nesupia had implemented, such as teaching English by playing games and having fun. She came from a strict teaching background in Canada and was used to more rigid methods. After a couple of weeks her employment was terminated. Then a young Australian teacher came with her ten-year-old son and stayed for two nights until she also disappeared. It is rather normal that teachers come and go working for an organisation like Nesupia in China. Several teachers during the year packed their bags and left during the weekend without telling anyone.

In March, Melly, a twenty-seven-year-old girl from New York with whom I had become friends, asked me to come along to "the English corner" at the Guangzhou Library on a Sunday morning. There are lots of English corners in China, where Chinese people can go and speak to English speaking people and practise their English.

It was rather overwhelming. I was there from 10 a.m. to 1:30 p.m. and was constantly surrounded by twenty to twenty-five people; old and young people as well as young children. You can easily feel like an important person in those surroundings. I think the Chinese people were interested in me because I looked so different, and they were fascinated by Australia.

There were only a few foreigners there, perhaps five or six. I had so many invitations to be taken around Guangzhou, and out for dinner, as they were so keen to improve their English. Many of the people said, "Please come back next Sunday; we like talking to you." I was told at least ten times that I was so beautiful. It was difficult for me to get used to all the compliments. But on returning to my apartment I would stand in front of the mirror telling myself, "You are just a normal person." It is very normal for foreigners to get a lot of attention in China.

After seven months without a computer at home (I had been using the computer at the Nesupia office) I decided to buy a second-hand computer. Peter and I went to the computer market and each of us bought a computer and a printer. It was no problem setting up the computer and printer in my bedroom, and I bought an Internet card so I could go online at home in my bedroom. I could also watch movies on the computer. A young teacher from Canada, Ray, came and helped me set up the speakers. For seven months I had written my travel journal in notebooks; now I could start writing on the computer.

It felt so good to be in my room, watching videos and listening to music. My room was so comfortable; I loved it. From the big bay window with a window seat there was a view over one of the many man-made canals that run through Guangzhou to take the overflow of water from the Pearl River in the rainy season to prevent flooding.

After studying Chinese once a week (paid for by Nesupia), I was happy that my language skills were improving. I still had a long way to go, but it was so exciting that I now sometimes understood when the students were speaking Chinese. One day, a little girl came running into the classroom and told me a long story in Chinese, which of course I could not understand. Instantly some other students came running over to her saying *"Ta bu ming bai"* (she doesn't understand). A few days later I picked up something from the floor to put it away and a boy came over and said, *"Wo da"* (that's mine), and there were many other situations where I would get so excited when I understood. It was also a thrill when I could say a sentence in Chinese and I was understood. Who would ever have thought that one day I would speak Chinese.
I was really enjoying this new learning curve.

I continued enjoying the teaching and how I was improving lesson by lesson. Experience is a wonderful thing. I felt happy and comfortable in the classroom, and the children liked me so much and responded to my teaching .

One day I was teaching a Grade 1 class about fruit. It was such a fun lesson. In the previous lesson I gave the students photocopies of fruit for them to take home to colour in. So this lesson we had to make "fruit salad" out of their different coloured-in fruit. So I asked, "Who has a pineapple?" and the student with the pineapple came up the front to cut up the pineapple (with scissors) and place the paper fruit in a beautiful plastic bowl I had bought for that purpose. Each student in turn came up with their paper fruit to cut up and place in the bowl.

After all the paper fruit had been cut up we played a fruit salad game and while we did that Jean (my TA) switched the bowl with the paper fruit with an identical bowl with real fruit salad (which I had brought as well) hidden under a towel.

So after the game I told the students that we had to eat the fruit salad and of course the students thought we had to eat the paper fruit. When I lifted the towel and they saw the real fruit salad in the bowl they got so excited. "How did Miss Tove do that?" they asked Jean.

Jean replied, "Oh, Miss Tove can do magic things!"

So we dished up the fruit salad in individual small bowls and gave the students a little plastic spoon to eat it with, and how they loved it. What a joy it was to see the expression on their little faces when they saw the real fruit salad. How wonderful it must be to be young and still believe in magic.

Five years later, my favourite little student Selina, who continued to be my student for the next nine years, asked me one day when we had lunch together, "Miss Tove, when I was in Grade 1 and you did the magic trick with the fruit, how did you do that?" I was amazed she remembered but also happy that it had made an impression on her. Of course I told her it was magic!

I was asked to do a presentation with my students for a group of high-ranking government officials who would be visiting Dong Feng Dong School. It was rather exciting to be asked. I practised a special presentation with the students but sadly the presentation was not what I had expected. All the officials came but they were thirty minutes late and only had thirty minutes to check over the school. They only took a quick glance into our classroom. It was disappointing for the students, as they were all dressed up in their beautiful summer school uniforms and looked so gorgeous. Jean and I made it up to them by playing games and having some fun.

I enjoyed teaching in the kindergarten on Saturday mornings. The students were delightful and I looked forward to those mornings.

At the end of each class I taught the students to line up in front of me, than we would march nicely out the door. The students all wanted to be the first in line, and so they would rush toward me to be number one. One Saturday morning, the competition was so fierce they grabbed hold of my slacks to try to be first in line, with the result that they all fell over. However, they didn't let go of their grip on my slacks and the result was they pulled my slacks down! At that time I had lost a lot of weight and so my slacks were loose on me. And there I was, standing in the classroom with ten little children around my feet and my slacks around my ankles!

I was worried I would fall on top of the children so I had to call my TA Kerry for help. As I was standing there with my slacks around my ankles I was thinking back to my childhood. When I was a little girl in the village in Denmark my mother told me, "Always wear clean underpants as you never know when you will get run over by a car and have to go to hospital." At that moment I thought of my dear departed mother and remembered her advice; I was so glad I had put on clean underpants that morning! My mother could never have known that one day her youngest daughter would stand in a classroom in China with ten children around her feet and her slacks around her ankles, being grateful for her advice!

11 EVERY DAY WAS AN ADVENTURE

This life is what you make it. – Marilyn Monroe

I was excited about making a trip to Hong Kong during the May holidays. In China, this holiday is the first week in May and it is called The Golden Week, as it is a time Chinese people like to go shopping and spending up big. Through another teacher, Heather, I got the name and address of a guesthouse in Kowloon called Star Guest House. I was told it was clean and cheap, and only $50 per night. I was able to phone and book a room. I decided to catch the bus as it was cheaper than the train. It was a bit of a hassle, as I had to get off the bus on the Chinese border, go through Chinese customs with my luggage, then get on the bus again, drive a few hundred metres and finally go through Hong Kong customs. I made a decision that next time I would catch the train, which was twice as expensive but much easier.

The bus stopped at the BP Hotel in Kowloon, which was in walking distance of the Star Guest House in Cameron Street. I found the street and Guest house easily. I was so happy to be in Hong Kong, which is often regarded as the most exciting city in the world. It was, as I expected, very Western and as I walked the streets in Kowloon it was certainly a much different sight from Guangzhou. There were so many different races and especially so many Westerners.

Hong Kong is also known as a shopper's paradise and I could see why. The shops were bulging with tempting goods but as I had lived on mainland China for nine months and was used to cheap goods, I didn't find Hong Kong prices all that attractive. All the famous brands from around the world were displayed in very expensive shops along Nathan Road (the main road in Kowloon).

I decided to play tourists and caught the double decker bus up to Victoria Peak; the view was spectacular over the gorgeous Hong Kong harbour. Often clouds cover Hong Kong and the spectacular view from Victoria Peak can only be imagined but I was lucky and had a splendid view on an almost clear day. I only spent two days in Hong Kong but it was enough for me to get a taste of this exciting city and I would return many times over the next many years.

和平

On my return from Hong Kong I became ill with a very high temperature, sore throat and chest cough, and stayed in bed for several days until I was so ill I knew I needed to see a doctor. Fortunately, it was still the May holidays, and so I didn't miss any teaching.

I asked one of the other teachers where there was a doctor or a hospital and she said there was a small hospital just down the street. I managed to get up the strength to walk down to the hospital. What an experience! My goodness! I never want to be seriously ill in this country, that's for sure. Arriving at the hospital I was met with giggles by a few nurses (which is normal). Young Chinese people get so excited to see a foreigner. Then they started arguing about who should deal with me! Finally, one spoke to me in Chinese, which I didn't understand, and they didn't speak English. To let them know my medical problem I coughed and pointed to my throat and chest. They seem to understand and so a phone call was made and the nurses gestured to me to go out the door with a young man. I had no idea where we were going. I followed this young man who walked very fast. I did not walk fast as I was really ill, and so he had to stop and wait for me often. We must have walked a kilometre through a little narrow street, and I was thinking. *Where are we going?* I felt like Hansel and Gretel wanting to throw breadcrumbs down to find my way back. In fact, I did get my notebook out to draw where I was being led just in case.

Finally we were outside another hospital; it looked okay, and the young man took me inside and motioned for me to go into a little room just inside the main door. When I got in there, I saw a very young man and a young girl sitting at a desk. When they saw me they started to giggle, as usual. I asked if they spoke English and they replied that they spoke very little. When I asked the young man if he was the doctor, I got a nervous "yes." He looked so young! Both the doctor and the nurse looked as if they were dressed up in their parents' clothes and playing doctors and nurses. When I told him I was sick, he said he'd try to help me.

Straight away I had no confidence in the doctor, as he didn't seem to know what to do. He moved paper around the desk a lot. I showed him in my phrase book what my symptoms were (I had already marked them down before I left home) like sore throat, chest cough, runny nose and headache. He finally got out from somewhere in the drawer of the desk an ice cream stick and checked my throat and told me to say "ahh." He then looked in the drawer again, which was almost falling apart, and found a stethoscope that had seen better days. He indicated he wanted to listen to my chest; the way he did this did not increase my confidence at all.

He then somehow found in his limited English vocabulary the word X-ray and gave me a piece of paper and pointed down an empty corridor. This hospital only had one other patient, an old woman sitting on a bed in the next room. The hospital was deserted. What had everyone else found out that I didn't know? Anyway, I wandered down the hallway and suddenly a man walked out of a room and motioned for me to come in and pointed to a step for me to stand on, I guessed as he was going to take an X-ray. It took thirty seconds and he then waved me out of the room again. I did not know what to do next. Having no choice, I wandered back to "my little doctor." He somehow had already been told my chest was clear. Thank goodness; I would have hated it if I had been seriously ill with a chest infection.

Then he wrote out a prescription for me for three different kinds of medication: one for my chest, one for my runny nose, one for my throat. There was a chemist shop in the hospital and so I could get my medication on the way out. I slowly made my way back to the main street, having noted down landmarks, as I did not have any breadcrumbs, and I got home safe and sound.

I didn't really have confidence in taking the medication. I checked with another teacher who had been in China for a couple of years and she said it looked okay. Whether it would help or not, who knows, but Chinese medicine is supposed to be excellent and the packaging inspired confidence. It was very securely packaged in three layers of cellophane.

It was an interesting experience and once again "T.I.C. This is China" was uttered while taking my medicine which was very much like Western medicine and fortunately after a few days I was healthy again.

和平

I could not wait to wake up in the mornings to begin a new day because every day was an adventure. I loved my slow morning start. I woke up when my eyes opened and not when the alarm clock went off. I showered and drank a beautiful brewed cup of coffee from a coffee machine that was a gift from a Canadian teacher, Lucy, who had left to go back home.

I strolled leisurely to my school, Dong Feng Dong School, at 9:45 to 10 a.m. I liked to give myself plenty of time, as I loved to stop along the way and observe, narrow alley life. I would take a shortcut to the school through narrow alleys where people still lived as I am sure they did one hundred years ago. On either side of the narrow alley were very old apartment buildings five to six levels high and small shops or cafes on the ground level. Some of the cafes were only the size of a cupboard or a tiny room where the owners (usually families) struggled daily to make a living. The cafes had a few tables and chairs inside, but mostly customers would sit on small stools on the footpath outside. The kitchen was in the corner and food preparation was either in full view of the customers (which was good, as we could see how the food was prepared) or indeed right on the footpath on a large wooden board. The food scraps and wastewater were just thrown out into the gutter.

As I walked past in the mornings, the café owners were busy preparing for the lunch trade, and many times I had to jump to avoid having a bowl full of dirty water thrown on my feet! I guess it was convenient for them just to throw the water into the gutter and not in the drain. I have been told there was very little checking on the health standards of those little eating places, and new ones would appear almost every day. It is so easy to set up a little eating-place and they may only last a few weeks or months sometimes. But the ones that provide good food keep going of course. Other food places were just in a door opening. The owner had only set up a skillet and a gas ring and was making pancakes with some sort of filling, noodles, *jiao zi* or similar food which was easy to cook. I would often stop at one of the little cafes to treat myself to a late breakfast of *jiao zi*, which I would pick up with chopsticks and dip in a delicious peanut sauce, or eat a bowl of freshly made noodles. If the *jiao zi* and the noodles had been boiled I felt safe eating them.

I always liked supporting small business. I found myself respecting those poor people working so hard to make a living. Many of the tiny cafés were open twenty-four hours a day.

There doesn't seem to be any structure to the shops. There are goldfish shops next to a shoe repair business, mobile phone shops and small take-away food places all mixed together. There are hairdressing salons galore. I have never seen so many hair dressing salons; there could sometimes be three next to each other, and they had so many staff members just sitting watching television during the day. However in the evenings the staff would become busy shampooing, cutting and styling hair.

和平

One day in spring I had an interesting experience walking home from school. I was walking along the canal which was absolutely filthy; imagine the most polluted water possible then double it. This canal was across the road from where I lived. I walked along that canal to get to the school. I suddenly heard screaming and shouting behind me. I looked to see what was happening and saw a man running across the road toward me followed by police officers and about half a dozen security guards. I realised the man had done something wrong. As the man was looking behind him at the officers, he didn't see me and ran straight into me—not hard; he just brushed me. As I was right alongside the canal I wondered where he would go. He then jumped over the railing and into the filthy canal! I screamed out, "Oh no!" and ran over to the railing to look and there he was half walking, half swimming across the canal to the other side!

It seemed as if the canal was not as deep as I had thought, and the filthy water only came up to his chest. A lot of people had gathered along the railing and they started to throw stones in the canal toward the man. I guess he thought he could get to safety on the other side but alas the police had obviously alerted the law enforcement on the other side of the canal (there are many police officers and security guards around all the time), and a few came running toward the canal on the other side where many people had also gathered. In fact, he could not have climbed out on the other side, as it was a straight wall. He started to swim toward a drain where the water ran into the canal (who knows what comes through that drain; I dare not guess) and he crawled into the drain like a water rat. I stood and watched for about ten minutes. It was interesting to witness such an event. Nothing else happened and so I walked home thinking about this. All the other teachers were so envious. Betty said it wasn't fair as she had been in Guangzhou for five years and had never seen anything exciting like that!

It was a Friday evening in April and I had spend the early part of the evening at the Reading Club which I had volunteered for at Nesupia (reading with clever students to improve their English). After reading class, I met up with a few of the other teachers to go to Larry's new workplace, which was a bar where he was the entertainment organiser. His job was to find bands to play in the bar.

We met in Jenny's apartment and I was drinking a lovely drink Jenny had bought called Cranberry Bacardi cocktail. One of the young American teachers arrived with "dope" and Jenny was worried how I would react and so she called me into the kitchen and said, "They are going to smoke a joint; would that offend you?" I replied that it wouldn't. I had never had any experiences with drugs and so I just looked at it as another experience to observe. It was interesting to see the young people roll the joint and they offered me "a drag," which I declined. I felt I had arrived at the age of fifty-eight without that experience and so I didn't need to try it now.

We then all got into a cab and went to the bar where we were sitting outside in the courtyard under the trees. It was an old house that had been converted into a bar. It was great as a lot of teachers were there and they were all happy to see me. They said how good it was to have me join them. They thought I was "so cool." I was drinking a beer which usually I *never* do. My life had changed. A good band was playing and we enjoyed sitting listening to the music. After a while we got up and danced. It was so much fun to feel young and alive again on the dance floor with the young teachers. I felt like the dancing queen in the Abba song.

After a while, Jenny and Larry wanted to go home and the others were going to another bar called Tang and wanted me to come. But I went home with Jenny and Larry, having had a great evening. I was worried I would wake up with a headache the next day but I didn't.

和平

A new opportunity came my way one day in May when Melly, the teacher from New York with whom I also had the "English corner" experience, approached me, asking me to go and have dinner with her, which I was happy to do. We went to a little local restaurant that served *jiao zi* (dumplings). She made me an offer that would once again change my life. She suggested we should start our own business working as freelance English tutors. For some reason she thought I would be a good partner.

Melly had researched the possibilities and was of the opinion that it would be easy to get tutoring jobs with companies or rich individual adults who wanted to improve their English. I liked the idea and immediately started to do the calculations to make sure I would have an adequate income. It would pay 150 RMB an hour ($25) and so in fact I only had to do three or four hours a day tutoring to achieve the same income I was on now, which was 8,000 RMB per month ($1,350) plus accommodations, which I valued at 2,000 RMB ($340). So I had to earn 10,000 RMB ($1,680) a month. I would have to find my own accommodations but Melly and I agreed that we would share an apartment and it would be possible to get a nice one for 2,000 RMB ($340) a month. As well as tutoring during the week, we would also be able to tutor on Saturday and Sunday, which was a popular time, as usually adults had the weekend off and children didn't go to school. So the opportunity to earn a lot of money was there depending on how many hours you wanted to work.

Melly had already made the arrangements for herself and started doing some tutoring for a wealthy businessman being paid 150 RMB ($25) an hour. I was able to monitor how she was going before I decided whether to stay in the secure job at Nesupia or move on. Melly would move into an apartment and I would then join her on July 9th if and when I finished at Nesupia.

I was a little worried, as it was an uncertain future, but I wanted to be brave and take a chance to do something different and challenging. I could stay at Nesupia and if I stayed, there would be some sort of security. But now I had realised there was so much money to be made in tutoring and for less work it was looking attractive to me. Most tutoring is not too taxing either.

In April and May, Melly and I continued our discussions and planning about the joint tutoring business we would set up together. I arranged interviews with several kindergartens and training centres and finally decided on a job for a training company called PQ where I could work as an English teacher for a few hours a week until I got enough tutoring clients to support me. At PQ I would be teaching adults and also teaching children weekdays late afternoon. PQ seemed like an excellent company. It had been established for over ten years and Paul (the owner) took a very personal interest in the running of the company. PQ offered me a contract with a twelve-hour work week schedule which was usually in the middle of the day between 11 a.m. and 3 p.m. I would be paid 5,000 RMB ($840) (or perhaps more) and 1,000 RMB ($168) living allowance which brought me up to 6,000 RMB ($1,008) for only twelve hours of work.

I was also offered a job at another training centre called Apex, which was run by a young Chinese/Australian man, and the first job he asked me to do was to teach English to the employees at the HSBC bank. I went to the bank to have a look but felt uncomfortable as it was just like the office environment I had left behind in Brisbane and I certainly didn't want to get back into that environment again. So my decision to accept the job at PQ was the correct one for me.

Even though the freelance future looked bright, I had decided I wanted to leave the door open to Nesupia. I wanted to leave on very good terms, just in case. I felt better having a safety net, so to speak.

In June, despite all our planning and research, Melly decided to return to the USA but as I had already done so much preparation I wanted to continue by myself. I just made some changes in my plans. I decided to devote Saturdays and Sundays to teaching children. I had a database of 300 students I was teaching in the primary school. That was the start of "Miss Tove's English School."

During the month of May, as well as continuing my teaching job with Nesupia, I also started working part-time for PQ Training College teaching young adults on Wednesday evenings. It was so different teaching young executives from teaching primary school children and it wasn't as enjoyable. The owner, Paul, liked to make a lot of money and so put fifty students in each class and I was supposed to teach conversational English! The class was one hour long, so that meant just a little over one minute for each student to have an opportunity to speak on a one-on-one basis. Most of the students were too shy to speak as they had only studied English in primary or high school in classes of fifty students, and so had no practice in speaking English. Despite this their written English and grammar was good. I was to learn that this is a very common situation in China.

The owner was getting so much positive feedback from the students about my teaching that one day he said to me, "What are you doing to the students? Everybody loves you!"

I just smiled and said, "I just like teaching." I told myself I had to be very careful I didn't let all the compliments go to my head! I had to remain humble.

The students were happy and excited to have a foreign teacher. A few of them were brave enough to come and talk to me after the class finished and I became good friends with two young girls named Rachel and Harriet and also a young man called Joey. Rachel and Harriet were university students. Joey was waiting for a sponsorship to go to the USA to study at a conservatorium of music. He was a very talented cello player.

I had many enjoyable hours with my new young friends. They enjoyed teaching me Chinese and about Chinese culture and in exchange they got free English lessons.

Many young people in China desperately want to become friends with foreigners so they can practise and improve their English. Many times I was befriended on buses or subways, and even on the streets, by young people who wanted to speak

English. It was rather flattering in the beginning until I realised they really just wanted to be my friend to improve their English.

Toward the end of the school year, lots of things were happening. Teachers were resigning one by one. It was a bad situation that so many teachers were leaving so close to the end of the school year. It meant so much work for the teachers left behind. Nesupia was not thinking of employing new teachers, as it was very close to the end of the school year. The end of the school would finish on July 9th but then all the teachers had to stay an extra two weeks to teach in the summer school.

I found it difficult to understand why the teachers would leave so close to the end of the school year, as they would lose the end of school year bonus, which was a considerable amount of money. This represented a month's salary and payment for sick days you hadn't taken, as well as return airfare. I certainly didn't want to lose that money.

In the middle of June, I handed out a letter of invitation to my students in Dong Feng Dong School to join my weekend English classes at "Miss Tove's English School." I asked certain students, the clever ones, to stay back in the classroom. I read out their names and they looked at each other as if to say, "What have we done?" Usually students were only asked to stay back in class if they had been naughty and noisy in class.

When the other students reluctantly left (they were wondering what was happening), I told the remaining students they had been held back because they were very special and clever students and that I would not be teaching them next year but I was giving them a special invitation to be tutored by me in my home. I told them I thought they had the potential to learn to speak English very well. Jean translated all this to them for me. They got so excited they could hardly sit still and wanted to rush to me to get the letter. A few little girls did come rushing over to me and hugged me and said, "I love you, Miss Tove." It was so touching. I felt so happy that I had such a wonderful response to the letter from the students.

Within the next few days I had about twenty-five positive responses from the parents. There were also other parents who had heard about it and came and asked if their children could attend my school.

Parents of students from other classes also came to see me to ask if their children could join my classes.

What I had not counted on was that some of the students had older or younger cousins (whom they call sisters and brothers, as they had no sisters and brothers due to the One Child Policy), and the parents wanted them tutored as well. I could see I would be very busy.

12 END OF SCHOOL YEAR

The whole art of teaching is only the art of awakening the natural curiosity of young minds for the purpose of satisfying it afterwards. – Anonymous

China's school year finished in the beginning of July and so in the month of June teachers are under a lot of pressure organising open classes for the parents to come and see their children performing—and they wanted to see their child performing perfectly. Chinese parents expect a lot from their children. I had ten open classes in the month of June.

Selina's mother, Helen, spoke to me after the open class and of course she wanted Selina to join my school. Helen invited me out for lunch the following day and over lunch she told me that she had inherited a language school (licence and premises) from her father which he had owned for forty years. Her father had left the school some time ago but she still had the licence (which is difficult to get in China). Helen wanted to start up the school again and offered me a job as English teacher. She knew, of course, that I was starting my own school and we discussed the possibility of her being the coordinator of my new "Miss Tove's English School." In exchange I would be her English teacher, helping her re-establish the language school. That was agreed and that lunch meeting cemented a strong partnership and friendship that would continue for many years to come.

At the end of the school year, Nesupia put on a performance of all the students in a large hall. Again the teachers had been put under a lot of pressure, as the students' performance had to be perfect. We had many rehearsals in the classroom and just one rehearsal in the large hall. All the teachers were hoping that on the night the students would behave, since during the rehearsal they had been impossible to control.

The teachers had to start the show by doing a performance. Two other Aussies, Simon and Janet, and I sang *Waltzing Matilda* and *Tie me Kangaroo Down*

Sport. Simon wore a swagman's hat and Janet had a swag, which is like a backpack. I had made a big kangaroo from cardboard to have on stage when we sang *Tie me Kangaroo Down Sport* and I had also made several cardboard boomerangs to throw out in the audience when we had finished singing. Other teachers would do something from their native country; the Canadians, for example, sang their national anthem.

We finished the evening with all teachers and students singing *I Believe I Can Fly* (a 1996 song by R. Kelly). We had been teaching the students the song during rehearsals in the previous weeks.

It was an excellent show and all the teachers were proud of the students. They performed very well indeed and the parents were happy.

On Sunday, June 27th, Jean had arranged a Chinese birthday party for me, with all my teaching assistants getting together at Jean's apartment and we would make *jiao zi* (dumplings)—and eat them, of course! She said she would make it a totally Chinese birthday party. It was my second time making *jiao zi* (I also made them in Beijing). It is very difficult to make pretty dumplings; it takes a lot of practice to encase the meat or vegetable mixture inside the little piece of pastry and press it closed so it looks pretty. Mine were not pretty, but they tasted good after they were cooked and it was a lot of fun. Jean also made me "long noodle soup." which is a must to eat on your birthday as if you do you are supposed to have a loooooong life.

The next day I asked Jean to join me for dinner at the exclusive a la carte restaurant at The Garden Hotel since it was the day of my birthday. We dressed up in our best clothes and jewellery. I even put on my diamond rings for the first time in China. I would never wear my diamond rings on the streets in Guangzhou, as there are many pickpockets and thieves. You stand out as a foreigner already and so wearing expensive jewellery is asking for attention from thieves. It was a wonderful evening with soft piano music playing in the background and delicious food and wine. Jean had never been to a five-star restaurant before and I loved seeing her enjoy herself. It was not expensive: the whole dinner with wine only cost $60 for two people.

The summer holiday in China is in July and August. Schools finish the first week in July and start again at the beginning of September. Chinese teachers give the students a lot of homework in their holidays, and so for the students most of the holiday is taken up with doing homework.

As many Chinese companies do not give their employees any holidays (only National holidays), parents do not get summer holidays to spend with their children. So they like to send them to summer camps to keep them occupied and also to improve their English, math, Chinese or they like for the children to learn a sport or play a musical instrument. Chinese parents certainly do not want their children to be lazy during the holidays. Perhaps the students may get one week's holiday where they can play or just laze about, or some students may just travel with their mother if she is not working. This was so different for me, as I was used to Australian children going to the beach and playing sports during their holidays.

As there is only one child in 99% of Chinese families, parents are also keen to organise their child getting together with other children so they are not too lonely during the holidays.

All teachers were obliged to "volunteer" for the two-week summer school. Many teachers didn't want to, as they were tired of teaching and wanted to either go home or travel. I was happy to do it even though I was tired, as I felt it would be a great teaching experience and it was well paid.

The teachers had been asked to write a suggestion for the English summer school program. I suggested the students should perform a play of the fairy tale *Rapunzel* (a German fairy tale written by the Brothers Grimm) and I was so happy that my suggestion was accepted.

I was then asked to write the script and with the help of the other teachers I put together the whole play. I also wrote the lesson plan, which I had never done before. I had to coordinate the props such as Rapunzel's tower in one corner, the Prince's castle in the other corner and the forest in the end of the classroom. There was also Rapunzel's parents' vegetable garden in the middle of the classroom with heaps of tomatoes. The tomatoes were cut out of red cardboard and we added a green leaf and it was laminated so it was very pretty. The vegetable garden was green leaves with different kinds of vegetables hanging on the vines. The office already had them, so thank goodness I did not have to make them! We had to make picture cards of Rapunzel, the prince, the witch, the mother and father, and also word cards to match the picture cards. The picture cards I found on the internet and we coloured and laminated them.

It all came together so well, and in just two days, I might add! The castle and the tower looked great; they were each about 2.5 m tall. The tower was dark grey and the castle was happy red and yellow. Everyone said our classroom looked the best. It was very satisfying, I must say. I didn't know I was creative and artistic. A great surprise indeed! All together it was a very valuable experience.

During the summer school we also took the students in big buses on a field trip to see a yoghurt factory called Yakult. The factory was very impressive. It was all stainless steel and immaculate. It was an interesting but tiring day, trying to stop the students getting too excited on the bus, getting them to sit still and stopping them from fighting. At one stage I had to sit between two boys who got into a fight and I took the hits, as they didn't stop hitting each other even though I forced myself in between them. "*Aiya*" (which is Chinese for "goodness gracious me")! Chinese children are really not any different from children in other countries.

The last day of the English summer school was a great day. I felt so relieved I had finished my first year as a teacher in China. I felt proud of myself as I had seen great results from my teaching and I received a lot of praise from the parents and also the Nesupia office staff. I was given an excellent reference.

I had already packed all my teaching material in a large box ready to return to the office, and on handing back the teaching material I was eligible to receive my last pay which was considerable. As I had not taken any sick days I received ten days' payment as well as a whole month's payment as a bonus. I was also reimbursed my return airfare between Brisbane and Guangzhou. I happily took the money and went to my apartment to pack and get ready for my new life as a freelance tutor and owner of "Miss Tove's English School." My heart soared like an eagle as I skipped down the street toward my apartment.

和平

Helen and I had met several times to arrange our partnership and as I had to leave the apartment provided by Nesupia, Helen helped me find a new apartment. It was wonderful to have her helping me, as I would never have been able to negotiate the real estate rental market by myself. I found a good apartment with a living room that was usable for teaching a small class of ten students. I had decided to restrict my classes to ten students so I would be able to give each student individual attention. I moved to the new apartment at the end of July and had the help of several of my Chinese friends. One of my friends had a car and so that made it easier. It was exciting to move to a new apartment and live like a real Chinese person instead of living in a building with all the other teachers. I felt so brave but I was happy to have the help of my TA, Jean, who had become a dear friend, as well as Helen. Helen helped me get the phone connected and arrange for water delivery. In China you *never* drink water out of the tap; you always drink water from bottles or have a large bottle of water delivered to your apartment with a water dispenser.

I settled into the apartment very quickly and I was happy there was a very secure lock on the door, as it was all very new to me. The apartment was on the 25th floor and so there were bars on the windows to prevent anyone accidentally falling out the window.

For some unknown reason I slept so much better in the new apartment than the old one; I guess in the old apartment there were a lot of young teachers who enjoyed the night life and kept me awake.

I enjoyed living in the apartment very much. However, one slight disadvantage was that the next door neighbour's window was at such an angle that they could look right into my living room and of course I could look right into theirs, so I needed to have my curtains drawn most of the time. One afternoon I heard terrible screaming and shouting from the apartment. It got worse and worse and I just had to go to the window to see what was happening because I was really worried. I looked through the window into the next door living room and I saw the husband and wife having a fight and then the husband got a grip around his wife's throat, squeezing tight until her face was very red. However, she was able to scream.

Fortunately she was stronger than him and fought him off. The fight lasted for a few minutes and during that time the old grandmother just sat there in a chair and simply didn't move. I felt so sorry for her. I was hoping she was blind and deaf. I was so distressed to be a witness to this and I wanted to help the poor woman but didn't know how. I couldn't phone the police, as I didn't know the number, and I didn't speak Chinese well enough. I wanted to knock on the door to the apartment but feared that the man would also attack me. I decided I would phone Helen to ask her what to do but then the noise stopped, thank goodness. I saw the man leave the apartment and the woman retire to another room. I was so relieved I could relax and enjoy my quiet evening. But I couldn't stop thinking about what I would have done had the fight not stopped.

In July I started teaching full-time (fifteen hours a week) for PQ as well as setting up my own school taking students on Saturdays and Sundays. At PQ I was teaching adults, and it was certainly different from teaching children. As I had a business and accountancy background, Paul, the owner, wanted me to teach business English. I must say I didn't enjoy it as much as teaching primary school and kindergarten children.

I had made lovely friends with some of my students I had taught over the previous month at PQ. They all wanted to be my friend and once again I had to be careful I did not spread myself too thinly. Three students Rachel, Harriet and Joey who had become special friends came over to my place one Sunday and we had a lovely day. Joey was a very cultured young nineteen-year-old and played the cello beautifully. I convinced him to bring his cello over to my place to play for me, which he did, and he was brilliant. He played all the classical pieces I love. I was moved to tears. He had spent one year at Shanghai's Conservatorium of Music and was home in Guangzhou for the holidays and used that time to improve his English. From the first day in the class he stood out as a delightful young man; I liked him instantly.

Joey had been told by his teacher at the Conservatorium in Shanghai that if he could improve his English and pass his TOEFL certificate, (Test of English as a foreign Language) they would help him get a scholarship to go and study in the USA. So I told him I would tutor him free of charge and help him fulfil his dream. I had received so much from this country and this city and it was one way I could somehow pay back for my wonderful experiences. He was so thirsty for knowledge and to learn English. It would give me the greatest pleasure to help him just a little to fulfil his dream to study in the USA and have the opportunity to travel to Europe to give concerts. I cannot remember ever before being so impressed by any young musician. He played with so much feeling. It was absolutely beautiful. It was another one of those times where I had to pinch myself and ask if this was really my life, sitting there in China listening to beautiful music filling the apartment. I closed my eyes and the music moved me to another space and time.

It was a coincidence that the evening before I had watched a TV program about a young Chinese musician who had become a world famous cellist. He was from Shanghai, his name was Wang Jian and he went to the same conservatorium as Joey. What a fascinating story! He was born in 1965 during the Cultural Revolution when Chairman Mao did not allow classical music to be played. Most classical music pieces, both written and recorded, were destroyed, but his father secretly made a cello for his son and Wang Jian practised in secret at home. He was self-taught and his father also helped him a little. So when Chairman Mao died in 1976 and the Shanghai Conservatorium opened again, he went for an audition and they discovered that, despite the hardships he had endured, he was indeed a very gifted child.

He was discovered by Isaac Stern (the famous violinist) who came to Shanghai in 1978 to give a concert. A documentary was made of Stern's concert, which was shown in the USA, and Wang was featured in that documentary. A couple in America saw the program and invited Wang to go to America to study with them, paying all expenses. Eventually, after much paperwork, he was accepted. It was a wonderful story. And what a coincidence that I should see that show and the next day this very gifted young cellist should come to my home and play for me! In fact, Joey knew Wang and had seen him many times as he often came home to Shanghai to teach at the Conservatorium.

Rachel and Harriet also enjoyed Joey's music. Harriet would be going off to university in September and Rachel was going into second year at University. I felt so lucky I had met such wonderful young Chinese people. They loved spending time with me. I had only expected them to stay for a couple of hours but they stayed all day.

The Olympic Games in Athens were in August and I tried to watch as much as I could on TV. I watched the opening of the Games and it was just wonderful. I loved how they combined the old and the new. I was very impressed. I eagerly followed the medal count and especially to see how many medals were won by the Chinese team.

I was talking to the students a lot about the Olympics in Athens and trying to get them excited about how well China was doing. I also talked about the Olympics in Beijing in 2008 and how proud they should be to have the Olympic Games coming to China. They did not seem to have as much pride in their country and the Chinese sportspeople's achievements as I would have expected. I seemed to be more excited about it than they were. I learned later as I continued my teaching in China that Chinese people are humble and they do not like to express pride in themselves and others. It is very common for Chinese people not to compliment others or themselves. I found this rather sad and I would include that in my discussions with my senior students and tell them it is okay to have self-pride and also to be proud of their country and countrymen who achieve great things.

13 FIRST ANNIVERSARY OF ARRIVING IN CHINA

Life is an opportunity, benefit from it. – Mother Teresa

In the month of August 2004 I had some sad news from Dagang in North China that Larry's father had died at the age of only sixty years. I remembered that kind, intellectual man who had welcomed me with open arms in February when I made my trip to the north of China. My heart was sad for his lovely wife who would miss her lifelong companion. It started me thinking about the possibility of my dying in China and I wanted to leave instructions for my daughter Elizabeth on what to do if this should occur. I was fifty-eight years old and my mother died when she was sixty. I hoped I would live for a long time yet, but I thought it was good to be prepared and for Elizabeth to know what to do if she must come to a strange country where she doesn't speak the language to make all the necessary arrangements.

和平

My little school was growing every week. More and more students came to my classes and I was also asked to teach in a kindergarten during the week. With the fifteen hours a week working at PQ, my income was very good. Helen also started building up her school and I would teach for her a few hours a week as well. I was amazed how much pleasure I gained from teaching in my own school, and it gave me so much satisfaction also to see it grow week by week.

As I had been in China for over a year, I was due for a dental check-up. I mentioned this to Helen and said I was worried, as I only wanted to see a dentist who spoke English. Helen found a dentist at a dental clinic called 'Smile' in an outer suburb of Guangzhou called Shunde.

The dentist, Dr. Wang, who spoke perfect English and was a very charming man, examined my teeth and recommended major work which I knew I needed as I had already been told by my dentist in

Australia. Due to my poor upbringing, toothpaste and toothbrushes were luxuries which the family couldn't afford and so my teeth had suffered and had been in bad condition during my adult years. Dr. Wang suggested I should get all my teeth capped and it would only cost a fraction of what it would cost in Australia. After considering it for a few seconds, I agreed. I got a quote which didn't scare me too much and I made several appointments in September to go ahead with the huge job.

I felt comfortable with the dentist, as he had good credentials. In fact, he was Chinese President of the International Academy of Integrated Dentistry, Vice-President of the Asian Academy of Aesthetic Dentistry and Vice-President of the Chinese Academy of Aesthetic Dentistry. At the conclusion of the many appointments to finalise the work I was so happy and grateful to Dr. Wang, as I now had a perfect smile. It was such a good feeling to finally get my teeth fixed and be able to laugh and open my mouth knowing I would show perfect teeth. Dr. Wang would continue to be my dentist for many years to come.

Through this dental surgery I was introduced to a Mongolian doctor who specialised in herbal medicine. I made an appointment to see him also in September. Apparently he could work out what my health problems were simply by taking my pulse! I wasn't too sure about that but I played along. He also noticed I had had a thyroid operation and wanted the history. He apparently was a specialist in thyroid complaints. He said (through an interpreter) that he could fix that problem permanently. I had so much attention in that doctor's room. At one stage, there were six doctors around me. The attention I was getting was at times uncomfortable. I was being treated like a superstar and I did not feel comfortable with that.

I agreed to try the permanent solution to my thyroid problem. Thirty-five years ago I had an overactive thyroid and 75% was removed and I had for all those years taken thyroid tablets to compensate for the loss of most of the gland. The Mongolian doctor gave me many different types of herbal medicine, beautifully packed in brown paper and labelled with names in Chinese script which I could not read. (But the instructions were translated into English for me). For the next few days I really tried to swallow the horrible bitter thick brown tea I had to drink but sadly I was unable to continue. I felt sick after each mouthful. So I said goodbye to Mongolian herbal medicine and continued my Western medication.

Even though I didn't like his medicine, the Mongolian doctor was an interesting man to meet. When I went in to see him he was dressed in his traditional Mongolian clothes: a bright yellow "garment" with matching scarf and cap. The traditional Mongolian garment is called a *deel* or *kaftan* and it is worn on both weekdays and special days. It is a loose gown cut in one piece with the sleeves; it has a high collar and wide overlaps at the front. The *deel* is tied with a sash. We had several photos taken of the two of us together. I was the first Western person he had treated and so I guess it was as exciting for him as it was for me.

The owner of the dental clinic had decided he wanted his staff to study English with me and so it was arranged that I come to the clinic once a week and teach the staff for one hour. It was difficult since there was a big difference in the English level among the ten staff members. But I made it work and they continued studying until the end of the semester. So in fact the money I earned from teaching English in the clinic almost paid for my dental treatment.

和平

I was invited to celebrate my second Mid-Autumn Festival with the owner of PQ Paul and his wife Cindy at a family gathering in their home. I went to the PQ office at 4 p.m. and we all got in the van to drive to their penthouse apartment on the 7th floor at Riverside Garden at Panyu. Panyu is a satellite city to Guangzhou. About 20 to 30 years ago farmland was bought from farmers and huge apartment complexes were built. Many families moved to Panyu to get away from the pollution of Guangzhou. We had to walk up seven flights of stairs—I was not impressed! Had I known that I would not have accepted the invitation! I am not fond of walking up and down many sets of stairs. However, it was a lovely and an interesting evening. The ladies were in the kitchen cooking and Paul and I watched the movie called *The Day after Tomorrow*. I had a wonderful massage in a massage chair while watching the movie. The massage chair would massage your whole back area and legs while you would just sit and relax, it was a wonderful feeling. I was told the chair cost 24,000 RMB ($4,000).

I could not believe what I saw when Cindy set the table. She put newspapers on the table as a tablecloth. I was surprised to see a tablecloth made of newspaper for a celebration as big as the Mid-Autumn Festival. After spending hours in the kitchen cooking many delicious dishes, the table was covered with newspaper! When we sat down to eat, I realised it was to catch all the food that people spat out while they ate. It was very interesting to watch how they put the food in their mouths and chewed and chewed, and then spat out whatever they did not want to swallow, like bones or whatever! In China meat is chopped up and cooked with bones and gristle and mostly the only way to eat the meat is to put it all in your mouth and then spit out what you do not want to swallow. Of course Chinese people do not eat with knives and forks, they just pick up the pieces of meat and other food with the chopsticks. I really do try to accept all cultures and habits, but this Chinese eating habit I found unpleasant. It was something that was taught. I had been out for dinner at expensive restaurants with families and I had seen the parents teach their children to do just that. This was so different from the eating practices Western parents teach their children.

Different countries have different cultures and I feel they must be respected. I am sure when Chinese people come to Australia they may find some of our practices different and perhaps unpleasant.

After we had finished eating I saw the sense of the "newspaper tablecloth." Cindy just took all the bowls and plates off the table and wrapped up the newspapers and threw them into the rubbish bin. Job done! No dirty tablecloth to wash!

After dinner we sang karaoke, which I had never done before, and it was interesting. Another teacher and his Chinese wife were there and she had a beautiful singing voice. We then ate some moon cake, which is a must at the Mid-Autumn Festival. I could only eat half a moon cake since they are so filling.

和平

As the Mid-Autumn Festival was a National holiday, I took the opportunity to go out and explore Guangzhou with my special young Chinese friends Rachel and Harriet. They arrived at 11 a.m. at my apartment so we could go out for the afternoon. It was lovely to see them and we spent some time talking. Harriet was telling me about her two weeks' military training she had attended before she went to university. It is compulsory for Chinese students, after they finish high school, to complete a two-week military course, which is very hard. One of the disciplines the students must endure is to stand in the hot sun for six hours and not move. Harriet had a very dark suntan which she really didn't like. Chinese girls are fanatical about keeping their skin pale. So she was looking forward to the tan disappearing.

We decided to go to Shamian Island and look around. It was wonderful to step onto the island, as instantly we left the hustle and the bustle of the Guangzhou street life behind. I heard birds singing and it was like being in Rome or Paris or another quiet area of a European city.

Shamian Island is a sandbar in the Liwan District of Guangzhou City. The island's name literally means "sandy surface" in Chinese. Surrounded by water, it is just like a giant ship mooring alongside the wharf. The island has been carefully planned. Three east-west avenues, Shamian Avenue, Shamian North Avenue and the South Avenue, and five north-south streets, Shamian Street 1 to Street 5 divide the whole area into twelve parts, with various buildings scattered around, namely the White Swan Hotel, Shamian Hotel and the Polish Consulate in Guangzhou.

The island has great historical significance. From the Song and the Qing Dynasties, it served as an important port for Guangzhou's foreign trade. Then it became a strategic point for city defence during the second Opium Wars (1856-1860). In 1859, the territory was divided into two sections, given to France and the United Kingdom (of which four-fifths went to the British and one-fifth to the French). Construction then took place including streets, drainage and imposing buildings and it became home to prosperous foreigners. From the late 1800s to the early 1900s, most of the public facilities were finished, including political buildings like consulates, cultural buildings like churches and schools, as well as commercial buildings like banks and firms.

After 1949, the mansions became government offices or apartment blocks and the churches were turned into factories as they were confiscated by the government. But after Chairman Mao's death they were restored, in many cases to their former splendour.

Each building has a label detailing its former purpose. A visitor can imagine what stories these mansions held while viewing the plaque outlining about its previous function. One example is "No.7 North Shamian Avenue," which was built during the Republican period and was formerly the

Administration Bureau of Broadcasting of the Nationalist Government. The mansions there form the best preserved western European style building complex in China. Out of the one-hundred and fifty buildings, forty-two are considered the most exotic ones in Guangzhou with Gothic, Baroque and Neoclassical architecture.

Since the early 2000s, the island has become well known for many Western couples staying there who want to adopt Chinese babies and young children, most of whom are female orphans. In particular, the White Swan Hotel, which has become a hotel of choice because of its convenient location for dealing with the bureaucratic aspects of adoption.

Shamian Island is a good place for a stroll. As it is just 900 m long from east to west and 300 m from south to north, you do not feel tired even after walking around the island twice. Due to traffic control on the island, it is a different atmosphere and pace of living. Problems such as traffic jams and exhaust pollution don't exist here. Now partly reserved for pedestrians, its broad boulevards are like long beautiful garden. Many expatriates are found in the bars and cafes on the southwest which have views over the Pearl River. Shamian Island would become my favourite place in Guangzhou in the years ahead.

With my two young Chinese friends, I walked around the streets along the river and through the lovely parks and arrived at the White Swan Hotel. We took a look around the hotel and also the bakery near the hotel which had delicious cakes and bread, catering for the many Westerners there.

We walked along a lovely path in a park and enjoyed watching the holidaymakers taking advantage of the holiday. I loved looking at the bronze statues that were all over Shamian Island depicting people doing everyday activities such as children playing, couples going for a walk, photographers taking pictures and old people sitting watching life go by. I was to learn later that the artist who designed the sculptures was the father of one of my students!

We also saw many couples enjoying ballroom dancing, as Chinese people love going to parks as often as they can to dance. In the evenings or on weekends you can see couples in any of the parks performing beautiful ballroom dancing to piped music coming from a tape recorder. Lots of Chinese people are involved in ballroom dancing competitions and even go to other countries to compete, and so it is probably much cheaper to practise in the parks than in halls or other venues.

We also saw many brides and grooms having their pictures taken in the lovely parks, near the fountains or the old buildings. I thought how lovely the brides looked in their Western wedding dresses. They looked like little China dolls. It is traditional that the bride and groom have their photo taken some time before the wedding. A huge photo is then displayed outside the ball room at the wedding reception at some time in the future. As we were watching the bride and groom having their photos taken, the bride had to change position and to do so she needed to lift up her long beautiful white wedding dress. We saw to our surprise that she wore jeans under her dress. It brought smiles to our faces.

Finally we arrived at a lovely little church and I realised it was a Catholic Church. Many people were decorating it for something special and I asked Rachel to find out what the special celebration was and we were told it was a wedding. We were then invited to come and watch the wedding, which was at 3:30 p.m.

How excited I was to actually see a Chinese Christian wedding. We continued our wander and returned to the church just after 3 p.m. to find that people were arriving for the wedding. I waved and said *ni hao* to the lady we had spoken to, who, I think, was the mother of the bride.

We went inside and found a seat down the back (out of respect, of course). We were there early and so we were able to see many of the wedding guests arriving. Many men had cameras and video cameras to capture the celebration.

Finally the groom arrived dressed in a cream suit with a gold tie and handkerchief in his pocket and black shoes. He found his place up near the altar, waited patiently for his bride and passed the time talking on his mobile phone!

Then the bride arrived, dressed in a lovely white full-length Western-style wedding dress with a veil covering her head and a long train. She was beautifully made up and had an elaborate hairstyle. To top it off, the most beautiful little flower girl and page-boy escorted her. They were so gorgeous! The girl really looked like a little doll and was beautifully made up and had a lovely hairstyle with a hairpiece of curly long pigtails. (As Chinese people do not have curly hair, they often attach curly hairpieces). The page-boy was dressed in a gorgeous "penguin suit" completed with tails and he also wore make-up: rosy cheeks and bright red lips. Nevertheless, he looked absolutely gorgeous. Their role was to walk up the aisle first and throw roses, which they did very well.

People in the church were looking at me wondering what I was doing there. They took many photos of me, capturing this funny-looking foreigner attending a Chinese wedding. When anyone looked at me I just smiled and said, "N*i hao*." An old Chinese lady sat behind me and told me (through Rachel as interpreter) that she lived close to the church and always came to watch the weddings. She was a Catholic and had her rosary beads in her hand. I would have loved to talk to her some more about what it was like to be a Catholic in China but the church was not the right place. I would need to find some other way to get that information. Rachel was very interested in Christianity and was so excited to be able to observe a real Christian wedding.

It was interesting to follow the church service in Chinese and, as I knew what the priest was saying, I could pick out a few words. It was amazing to see a young Chinese man dressed as a Catholic priest. He looked so young, about sixteen or seventeen years old. Of course he would have been older but the young Chinese men often look very young. The church service and the wedding service were just like in a Western church and the bride and groom left the church followed by the family, and the father of the groom was dressed beautifully in a Chinese jacket and the father of the bride was dressed in a Western suit. Wedding photos were taken outside the church. It seemed that the traditional Chinese wedding was being replaced or at least influenced by Western customs.

The bride and groom saw me as I came out of the church and reached out to touch me. I really didn't feel it was my place to become involved in the wedding and to get close to the bride and groom as I was only an observer, but I allowed them to touch me and I said, "H*en piaoliang*" (very beautiful).

After this lovely experience, we walked off the peaceful island to catch a bus to get home in the 5 p.m. traffic, which creates many traffic jams. But I have learned just to relax and go with the flow. There is nothing you can do and so the best thing is just to enjoy the interesting street scenes—and there are lots of them. It was my first time on one of the electric buses. In Guangzhou they have both electric buses and normal buses that run on fuel. The electric ones are slower but I felt good about not (at least for a short time) contributing to the huge pollution problem in Guangzhou.

I got home very tired but happy after a wonderful day. The weather at that time was perfect. It was not too hot—around 25-26 degrees Celsius. In spring and autumn the weather in Guangzhou is ideal.

Another day during the National Holiday period, I had arranged to meet another ex- student, Jan, who lived on Shamian Island and worked at the famous Victory Hotel on the island. We went to the Victory Hotel and had lunch; Jan suggested I should try pigeon and I reluctantly agreed. I am sorry I agreed, as it wasn't very nice and I really didn't feel comfortable eating a pigeon. The bird was so tiny and there was hardly any meat on its tiny body or legs. It was mostly bones.

We also had fried rice and three different *dim sums*, one type of rice pancake rolled up, another type of dumpling with meat inside and something like a spring roll with some meat inside. There was a lot of food left over and we got a "doggy bag" each, which I was glad about as I didn't want Jan to waste her money. She had insisted on paying for the lunch.

Over lunch Jan told me the interesting story of her life. Her grandfather was from Malaysia and had come to Guangzhou with his Malaysian wife. They lived in Guangzhou for a while and then went back to Malaysia where her father was born.

Her grandfather then wanted to come back to Guangzhou in the early stages of the Cultural Revolution but his Malaysian wife didn't want to, and so he returned with his son. He later married a Chinese woman and when Jan was born in 1971 her parents were separated and had to go away to work. This was during the Cultural Revolution and they were sent out to the countryside to do hard labour and her grandparents brought her up. That was a very normal situation during the Cultural Revolution from 1966 to 1976. The parents were sent away to the country to work and the children were brought up by the grandparents. It must have been so difficult for everyone involved.

In the early 1950s, the grandparents had been given an apartment on Shamian Island because the government had confiscated a huge mansion from some wealthy people and divided it up into apartments which were given to workers. Jan's grandfather worked for the local newspaper.

Because of the Cultural Revolution, Jan now lives right in the heart of this beautiful island. I was so excited that I now knew someone who lived there. Jan's husband is an engineer; he builds roads and works away most of the time. He only comes home for a couple of days once a month.

The Victory Hotel is a very old hotel which has just been restored. Jan had worked there for twelve years. She showed me around the hotel and the foyer as well as the rooms were very beautiful indeed. The hotel had a very strong Italian and Greek style with old paintings on the wall and murals of Greek dancing ladies. It was a delightful day with new experiences and stories.

On the way home, I had a lovely encounter with a young American girl who sat next to me on the subway. She was from North Carolina and was a missionary in Guangzhou together with her whole family: mother, father, three sisters and four brothers. She told me that her name was Joy (middle name Elizabeth) and her sisters' names were Grace, Hope and Faith. I was expecting her to tell me her brothers' names were Jesus, Peter, John and Paul but she disappointed me— they had names like Chad, Lindsay, Geoff and George!

She was a pleasant young girl, very tall with long curly hair. I was interested in finding out what it was like to be a missionary in China so I gave her my email address and hopefully she will keep in touch and give me some information. She said her mother was writing a monthly newsletter to their friends back home calling it "My life in China" and she said she would ask her mother to add me to her email list. I was able to find out there are many missionaries in China but they must work in secret, as if they are found out the government will send them back home and they will never be allowed into China again.

14 EMBRACING LIFE AND ALL ITS CHANGES

The purpose of life is to live it, to taste experience to the utmost, to reach out eagerly and without fear for newer and richer experience. – Eleanor Roosevelt

Our summer said goodbye and autumn said hello. I like autumn and spring. I am not fond of the winter in Guangzhou, as it can get a little too cold for my liking. Summer is very hot—between 30 and 36 degrees Celsius—and this summer just passed I did not save on air conditioning. I made full use of it and couldn't survive without it. The previous winter was very cold and so I was hoping that coming winter would be a little milder. Hopefully it would come late and leave us with wonderful autumn weather to enjoy a little longer.

My everyday life in this mysterious land of China was amazing. Every day I went outside my door was an adventure. I was being treated as a superstar wherever I went and everybody was so kind and helpful. I am sure all foreigner experience this when they come to China. Chinese people love foreingers. I felt so spoilt and wondered how I would ever fit into Australian society again being treated as a normal, average person. However, I did get a taste of being "normal" when I went to Hong Kong. No one there looked at me twice or came running up to me all excited, wanting a photo with me. The first few hours in Hong Kong got me right back to reality and I realised I am just like everyone else, which is good for me. It is easy to be lulled into a false sense of importance in China with all the fuss made of you.

One day I had an interesting experience being asked to do a television commercial. I was "spotted" while doing my grocery shopping in a large supermarket near my home. A young man from an advertising agency approached me asking if I was interested in doing a TV commercial. Of course he first said, "You are very beautiful." I am sure he says that to everybody.

I had also been approached a few months earlier and was offered a job in a TV commercial. I was walking down the street and was approached by the manager of an advertising company. He had seen me in the street several times and one day he offered me a modelling job in a TV commercial. The payment for one day's work was 1,500 RMB (about $250). Unfortunately, I didn't take the job as I didn't have time.

Another day I was again spotted in the street and asked if I wanted to be an extra in a movie being shot in Guangzhou. I said yes, as I thought it would be a fun experience. Steven Spielberg would of course be there, see me and snap me up for his next movie, I thought! In China anything is possible. Sadly, the project did not go ahead and so there was no stardom for me!

Anyhow, the young man who spotted me in the supermarket gave me his card and I gave him my card, expecting it would be the end of the matter but I received a phone call a few weeks later asking me to do a commercial. I was told it would be a very easy assignment, which paid extremely well; almost as much as I was paid per week in my old job in Brisbane, so a significant amount of money. It would only be a photo shoot and not a speaking part.

We had to travel to Shenzhen, the city on the border between Mainland China and Hong Kong, which was a train trip of about an hour. I had wanted to visit that city for a long time and so I was happy for the opportunity to become familiar with the famous Chinese city. Shenzhen is located in the southern part of Guangdong Province on the eastern shore of the Pearl River Delta. It borders the Pearl River Delta and Hong Kong. Shenzhen's location gives it a geographical advantage for economic development and in 1980, the first Special Economic Zone of China was built in this city. From then on, the city became the highlight of China and is well known for its rapid economic growth. More than thirty years ago, Shenzhen was just a small fishing village called Baoan County. In 1979, it was renamed Shenzhen City and now it is one of the most important financial centres in China.

I was told I would stay in a four-star hotel with all expenses paid and also that the commercial would take about one and a half days to film. My part was that of a wealthy woman sitting in her luxury apartment missing her daughter and looking at photos of her daughter. The commercial was to promote a new electronic speaking photo frame. They had found a beautiful Russian girl from Vladivostok in East Russia, Vera, to play the part of my daughter. Vera had long, curly hair and a very pretty face. Vera and I met the young man from the advertising company at Guangzhou railway station to travel by train to Shenzhen together.

What a fascinating experience it was! It reminded me of the movie *Lost in Translation*.

We spent the first afternoon taking still shots. The next morning, we got on a big bus with the director of the commercial and a large number of crew and made our way to a very nice part of Shenzhen, where we were going to use a living room in a luxury apartment for the filming. It was so fascinating to see the movie set take shape because it was indeed a movie set with tracks for the camera to roll on and many lights and it is *very* hot under those lights!

So we had to be made up for the part and I had brought several different kinds of outfits so the director could choose the appropriate colours and style he wanted. To our surprise, Vera and I were given a script and told to memorise the words; it was a three-page conversation between me and Vera as mother and daughter. We actually only had a few minutes to memorise the three pages before the director decided to start shooting.

The script was very poor English, which I pointed out to the agent, and so I got the job of editing the script. I also became the "unofficial advisor" on the set, as it was a Western setting and they wanted to make sure everything in the luxury living room was totally Western. I found it easy to act out the part, as I was in fact just acting myself, keeping my daughter Elizabeth in mind and missing her. However, Vera, my Russian daughter, found it difficult to act out her part; I think she was very nervous. I was asked by the agent to help Vera become more comfortable in her role. So in fact I was a very important person for *one day*.

The instructions we received from the director were confusing, as he could not speak English and my Chinese was restricted to understanding simple words and short sentences—not long, complicated sentences—and so it was very much body language. I learnt to pick up words from the director like *"bu hao"* (not good), and *"hen hao"* (very good). I liked it very much when I heard *"hen hao."* But very often they all forgot that I didn't understand much Chinese and I had no idea what was happening, so I just sat there with a permanent smile on my face saying, "What's happening? Someone tell me. Is this a *'bu hao'* or a *'hen hao'*?"

We started shooting at 9 a.m. and didn't finish until after 11 p.m. It was too late to catch a train back to Guangzhou and so we had to catch a taxi. The train trip was just over one hour and so the taxi would be expensive. It took a long time to find a taxi driver who would drive us to Guangzhou, as of course he wanted to make sure he could get a fare back to Shenzhen. But finally we were lucky and found a taxi driver who had just brought a businessman to Shenzhen from Guangzhou and so he was happy to take us home.

When I got back to my apartment in Guangzhou I had to stand in front of the mirror and remind myself that I was just a normal person as I had been treated like a movie star all day or indeed for a day and a half.

Since that time I was asked to do other commercials but I refused. It was fun to try it once but I did not have time, as I had to teach my students every day. Also, I was sure it would become boring work after the novelty wore off. The agent told me that I could earn a lot of money doing commercials. But in fact I earned twice as much teaching, and so the money didn't tempt me. But I had certainly developed a deep respect for actors, as I now knew what they have to go through to make a movie. I was only on the set for one day and I thought about them being on the set for months at a time.

和平

A few months after I started "Miss Tove's English School" I had so many students that my apartment was getting too small. Helen suggested that I move into an apartment she owned in the middle of the city of Guangzhou. It was a three-level penthouse apartment. The first level of the penthouse was on level 21 with a huge living room, a bathroom and a large kitchen with a window. In China many apartments have kitchens with no window, so this was luxury. The first level would be perfect as my classroom. On the second floor were two bedrooms; a large bedroom with a bathroom and a smaller bedroom. The large bedroom would be mine and the smaller bedroom I would convert into a living room.

On the third level was a very large balcony which would be great for playing games with the students. There was no furniture or curtains in the apartment and so Helen would furnish and install curtains for me. The apartment was very close to the subway station Ti Yu Xi Lu and Teem Plaza, the biggest shopping complex in Guangzhou, and it was right in the middle of the most prestigious business area in Guangzhou called Tian He.

During the month of November I was becoming very unhappy at PQ, as Paul, being impressed with my teaching, was asking me to teach more and more hours. I was not able to spend as much time expanding my own school as I would like. He was breaking my contract, as my contract stated I would work fifteen hours during the week and *not* Saturday and Sunday. But he wanted me to teach Saturday and Sunday as well. So after a discussion with Helen, we decided that I should resign from PQ and focus on my own school and help Helen expand her school as well.

It was not easy to resign from PQ but I had a choice to make and I made it. It later proved to be the right choice. Sometimes we have to make tough decisions, especially when we are in a new situation. I knew that what I was about to do may not work, but I found the inner strength, and the support of people like Helen to take that crucial step, which would set me up for the future. I could have taken the easy road where there was more certainty by staying with PQ, but my life had changed so much since I left Brisbane, so why not take this bold step?

I had passed the first anniversary of my arrival in China. It was amazing how quickly the year had passed! I was so happy and satisfied in my new life and hoped it would stay like that for many years to come.

Sitting at the computer, I was very tired after a full day of rewarding but exhausting tutoring. I was reflecting on my life over the previous year and reading a well-known quotation by Ralph Waldo Emerson, which my daughter, who was coming to visit soon, had sent to me:

The success of life.

Success is to laugh often and much - **which I do**
to win the respect of intelligent people - **which I have**
to win the affection of children - **which indeed I have**
to earn the appreciation of honest critics - **which I have**
the betrayal of false friends - **which I guess I have**
to appreciate beauty - **which indeed I do**

to find the best in others - **which I always try to do and have done even more so in China**
to leave the world a better place - **which, through my teaching and tutoring, I am sure I will**
to know even one life has breathed easier because I lived - **I dearly hope this is the case.**

I guess if I should die tonight it can be said I have lived a successful life.

Still, in my quiet moments, I could not believe how far I had come in a year and how so many of the wounds inflicted on me by the corporate world in Brisbane over the previous few years had healed. How I endured that time is beyond my comprehension but the human spirit can bear the most amazing punishment. But how grateful I am to have had this wonderful experience and found the beauty in life I had sought for so long.

In my darkest moments and my deepest despair, my daughter was always my tower of strength; she was the light at the end of the dark tunnel. She was then and still is "the wind beneath my often broken wings," and for that I love her so very much.

I can't wait to see what the coming years in China bring as the future is wide open for me at this point.

To be continued!

AUTHOR'S BIO

Tove Vine was born in Denmark into a poor family; she was child number 11 of 13 children. During her childhood there was a great deal of hardship, as it was often difficult for her parents to provide the necessities for the family. Due to the financial hardship, Tove had to leave school before her 15th birthday and make her own way in the world working as a maid and factory worker before obtaining a three-year apprenticeship in a large company and studied for a business college diploma part-time.

At age 19 she ventured to London, where she worked as an au pair for a wealthy Jewish family and met her future Australian husband while on holiday with the family on Jersey Island in the English Channel. Three years later she immigrated to Australia, where she married and had one daughter.

The years in Australia were spent in Newcastle, Townsville and Brisbane working as a beauty consultant, a business owner and later as an accountant. Due to her lack of education, Tove never stopped studying in her spare time as a mature-aged student.

In 2003 Tove (now divorced) decided to change her life completely, selling most of her possessions and moving to China to become an English teacher. She wanted to fulfil a childhood dream of becoming a teacher and also wanted to live in China.

After one year working for an English training centre, Tove established her own school called "Miss Tove's English School."

PHILANTHROPY

Because Tove knows the heartbreak of not being able to obtain a high school education, she feels passionately about helping to educate poor children. During her holidays she travels to teach English as a volunteer in orphanages in Asian countries. Tove has also established the Nepal philanthropy project which includes supporting the education of poor children. While teaching as a volunteer in Kathmandu, Tove also started "Miss Tove's Hygiene Program" which provides soap, handtowels, toothpaste, as well as toothbrushes, and teaches poor children to wash their hands before they eat to prevent sickness, as well as brushing their teeth. She also supports poor children in Nepal and in a mountain village in Guizhou (China) with second-hand clothes, toys and books which she collects from her Chinese students.

While teaching as a volunteer in an orphanage and helping out in a Charity Hospital in the Mekong Delta, Vietnam, Tove saw the need to establish a library in the Charity hospital to supply reading material for the poor, sick patients, as well as toys and children books for the sick children who had to spend time in the hospital.

Tove is donating 20% of the profit of the sales of her books to support and expand her philanthropy work.

Tove's motto is: "If I can help I must" – so everywhere she travels and she sees help is needed she helps.

Should you wish to help Tove expand her Philanthropy Project and sponsor a poor child in Nepal Please contact her on tovevine28@gmail.com

http://www.travelblog.org/Bloggers/Tove/
https://www.facebook.com/Tovevine
http://www.tovevine.com

100% of the donation will go directly to the child. There are no administration costs.

Glossary

和平 - *Hépíng* – Peace
Pǔ tōng huà - Mandarin
Guangdong Hua - Cantonese
Laowei - *foreigner*
ni hao - hello (direct translation you good)
piaoliang – beautiful
bu rou – no meat
mah-jong – Chinese game
bu hao – not good
hen hao – very good
wo bu ming by – I don't understand
hen piaoliang – very beautiful

Printed in Great Britain
by Amazon